THE NONPROLIFERATION PREDICAMENT

THE NONPROLIFERATION PREDICAMENT

Edited by
JOSEPH F. PILAT

Transaction Books
New Brunswick (U.S.A.) and Oxford (U.K.)

Library of Congress Catalog Number: 85-975
ISBN: 0-88738-047-6 (cloth)
Printed in the United States of America

Library of Congress Cataloging in Publication Data
Main entry under title:

The Nonproliferation predicament.

1. Nuclear nonproliferation—Addresses, essays, lectures.
I. Pilat, J.F.
JX1974.73.N67   1985   327.1'74   85-975
ISBN 0-88738-047-6

To my loving parents

Contents

Acknowledgments

The idea for this volume was generated when Dr. Irving Louis Horowitz asked me to compile and update a series of original articles on U.S. nonproliferation policy and to commission additional pieces for a companion volume. The collection of articles that originally appeared in the September/October 1983 issue of Transaction/SOCIETY were highly received, leading to Dr. Horowitz's suggestion that I obtain updated versions of the original essays and compile the new work.

I am deeply indebted to Dr. Horowitz and to the staffs of both Transaction/SOCIETY and Transaction Books for their unwavering assistance throughout the two publication processes. Scott Bramson and Dalia Buzin were particularly helpful in preparing this volume.

The magazine project began while I was still with the Congressional Research Service of the Library of Congress, where I benefited from the support and encouragement of Warren Donnelly and the production assistance of Gail Tate and Annie Littlejohn. And the book project received the expertise and encouragement of Donald Kerr, James Williams, and Steven Maaranen of Los Alamos National Laboratory. I would also like to thank Janie Kelly, who provided vital assistance in preparing the manuscript for publication, and Pauline Baca and Jan Dye, who supplied considerable production support.

Introduction: The Nonproliferation Predicament

Joseph F. Pilat

During the Eisenhower and Kennedy administrations, the prospect of a proliferated world posing the gravest possible dangers to U.S. and global security appeared imminent. It was expected that by the 1970s or 1980s there would be over twenty nuclear-weapon states. In the early 1980s, however, there are only five declared nuclear-weapon states; one state that has tested a nuclear explosive device hailed as a "peaceful nuclear explosion"; one state, possibly two states, believed to possess nuclear weapons or the capability immediately to fabricate them; and perhaps six "problem states," which are believed to be developing a nuclear weapons capability through their peaceful nuclear programs. At the same time, well over a hundred states have formally renounced nuclear weapons and there is arguably a general predisposition against further proliferation throughout the world.

If proliferation has not been prevented, it appears to have been managed during the last three or four decades. On the face of it, in light of the lessons of military history, this is simply astounding. It is now forty years after the first demonstration of an advanced military technology that has literally altered the course of world history, yet only relatively few states have sought to exploit the military atom and, of them, only six states have demonstrated a nuclear explosive capability. Even more surprising is the formal renunciation of nuclear weapons by states whose advanced civil nuclear industrial base has clearly given them the technological capacity to develop nuclear weapons. Virtually all of the advanced industrial states of the West have such a capacity.

Shall we attribute this situation to the self-sacrificing behavior of certain states, motivated by global and humanitarian rather than solely national inter-

1

ests? Perhaps, but if a principled opposition to nuclear weapons and their further proliferation may have been a motivating factor for some non–nuclear-weapon states, less exalted but quite understandable interests have driven others. It appears that for most, perhaps all, of the non–nuclear-weapon states, their status has been chosen or accepted as a consequence of political, economic, or technological limitations; the nuclear guarantees of a superpower; a relatively benign security environment; or an understanding of the instability and ultimate insecurity that could result from nuclear weapons if they invite the hostility or even the preemptive actions of the superpowers or regional antagonists, or generate a regional arms race.

To the extent that the denial of nuclear weapons was not influenced by principle or by national security interests, it was the effect of the operation of the international nonproliferation regime. The child of U.S. initiatives, reflecting the Atoms for Peace idea of international commerce under safeguards, this regime comprises treaty commitments proscribing acquisition of nuclear weapons; an international organization to verify no-nuclear-weapons pledges and to monitor peaceful utilization of nuclear materials and facilities; and a network of formal and informal agreements, both bilateral and multinational, that provide guidelines or establish conditions for nuclear trade and cooperation.

On general principles and policy prescriptions, impressive continuity and stability mark this international nonproliferation regime. And, there is an abiding belief in the United States and abroad that the regime is legitimate and necessary, and provides a more or less sound foundation for nuclear export and nonproliferation policy. Nevertheless, the regime is not monolithic. There are differences among U.S., European, and Japanese nuclear supply and nonproliferation policies, which are in turn different from those of important Third World states, some of which remain outside the regime. Nor is the nonproliferation regime static. It has evolved over the decades, in response to pressures from trends and events that threatened the objective of nonproliferation. As the regime continues to evolve, will it continue to be responsive to the problem of proliferation? Or will it become superannuated by new technologies, or enmeshed in and enervated by domestic and international political controversies and conflicting interests? What nonproliferation policies are likely to be effective in the 1980s and beyond, as states continue efforts to establish and to expand nuclear industrial bases, which could provide them with capabilities useful for the pursuit of weapons options in the future? Have the stagnation of the international nuclear market and the difficulties of nuclear threshold states like India given reasons for hope? Or will the limited proliferation of the past prove to have been a passing anomaly in military history, and the future be unlike the past?

Each in its own way, the papers of the academics, analysts, and policymakers assembled in this volume address these questions. While the questions are perhaps perennial, the responses they demand are definitely bound by time. And, although a plethora of papers and other writings attempted to answer these questions for the 1970s, this volume approaches them from the vantage of the 1980s. In light of the diverse perspectives reflected in our papers, the broad harmony of opinion on the objectives of nonproliferation policy is significant. There are challenges to the principles upon which the nonproliferation policy of the United States and the international nonproliferation regime is founded, but virtually all of the authors are supportive of nonproliferation efforts in the United States and abroad, while suggesting that adaptations and adjustments will be required in the years ahead if we hope to continue to curb the spread of nuclear weapons as successfully in the next decades as in the past four decades. Indeed, there appears to be a general consensus among the contributors that existing policies and institutions will have to be improved if the nonproliferation regime is to remain viable, and the idea of regulated and responsible supply is to serve the world of the future. But there are notable disagreements on how best to proceed, and evident tensions over desirable directions of present and future nonproliferation policy.

First and foremost, we see vestiges of the two traditional schools of thought on the relationship of proliferation to nuclear supply, students of which have historically advocated divergent policy approaches. The old boundaries have been blurred, but they do persist. On the one hand, those who hold that nuclear weapons proliferation is directly linked to the spread of nuclear material, equipment, and technology favor a technical approach. They seek above all else to clarify ambiguities in "trigger lists" and to make these lists and similar controls over nuclear supply more comprehensive, and more restrictive. On the other hand, those who view proliferation primarily as a political problem, only indirectly related to nuclear supply, take a different line. They seek to improve both supply and security assurances, and to refurbish existing, or establish new, institutional means to do so. And they strive to make supply relations more universal, and cooperative.

We also witness differences over the nature and scope of the changes perceived to be necessary. Some of these differences are profound, for they touch on principle. On one side stand those who believe current policies are basically adequate and who wish to avoid any disruption or erosion of the regime that might follow from initiating radically new policies or institutions. On the other side are those arguing for alternative nonproliferation mechanisms, and perhaps for new initiatives in the nuclear energy or arms control areas. The latter include those who believe that actions need to be taken immediately to deal with the concrete problems of the regime, and to restore the confidence in nuclear supply upon which it depends. However, they believe, too, that such modest, incremental measures will not be sufficient in the long term and argue that new solutions will be required in the coming decades to address proliferation risks posed by new supply conditions, as well as by the emergence of new nuclear technologies and new supplier states. Some who argue for major changes also challenge the scope and structure of what they view as an intrinsically inadequate nonproliferaton regime.

Whether piecemeal or sweeping measures to maintain and strengthen the nonproliferation regime in the future are advocated, it is clear from our papers that there is significant tension over the thrust or direction of these measures. There are differences over whether nonproliferation measures should be limited to nuclear export mechanisms or should utilize a panoply of economic, political, and even military instruments. And, questions over whether the measures are to embody a unilateral or multilateral approach, or be promoted by unilateral or multilateral action, remain controversial.

However broadly we define the proliferation problem, or the measures to minimize or prevent the further spread of nuclear weapons, the nonproliferation regime is at root a regime of regulated supply. It reflects historical hopes for the peaceful atom, as well as long-standing concerns in the United States and abroad that the expansion of nuclear power programs around the world poses proliferation risks. Accordingly, the health of the existing regime is contingent upon perceptions of the benefit and opportunities offered by peaceful application of nuclear energy, and there is considerable tension over the desired level of global commitment to nuclear energy in the future. Some hold that nuclear energy will be a crucial, perhaps dominant, element in any future energy "mix." Others, if they are not adamantly antinuclear, argue that we cannot phase out existing nuclear programs and should not foreclose opportunities provided by nuclear energy. But they assert that we have rushed pell-mell toward nuclear energy without recognizing that for technical, economic, or societal reasons, its benefits are limited.

In this vein, we also see evidence of disagreement over current and future policy implications of attitudes toward sensitive nuclear materials and technologies. The necessity of selective denial, either to certain countries or of certain sensitive items, is not a matter of general consensus. To be sure, rarely does anyone explicitly deny the necessity of using discrimination in the transfer of reprocessing and enrichment facilities and technologies. The question of whether to make enriched uranium and separated plutonium available to states that have an apparent need for these materials for advanced research or power programs is, nevertheless, disputed. On the one hand are those who argue that dispersal of these products exacerbates the dangers of nuclear proliferation and terrorism, and that their spread should be severely restricted. On the other hand are those who wish to make sensitive nuclear materials available under appropriate safeguards, arguing that only this will keep other countries from developing sensitive nuclear technologies themselves.

Are we likely to see a timely resolution of these competing perspectives and the policy approaches they suggest? Which perspectives on the risks associated with peaceful applications of nuclear power—and with nuclear cooperation and trade—are likely to prevail? What strategies for preventing proliferation are likely to be emphasized? No one school of thought is likely to gain total ascendancy, and no single nonproliferation strategy is likely to prove sufficient. These uncertainties, complexities, and ambiguities are troubling, but they are not unprecedented. The predicament they present has been evident in past nonproliferation policy. If it has not yet totally undermined the regime, as the surprising inaccuracy of official forecasts of future proliferation during the 1950s and 1960s suggests, can we be assured of the regime's survival in the face of today's and tomorrow's challenges? Confronted with this persistent nonproliferation predicament, will our wisdom or our good fortune triumph during the next four decades? Or, will we witness the emergence of the proliferated world predicted during the past forty years?

1

Common Sense and Nonproliferation

Richard T. Kennedy

Since the dawn of the nuclear age nearly four decades ago, the United States has been firmly commited to the objective of preventing the spread of nuclear weapons. That principle is embodied in the Nonproliferation Treaty (NPT), support for which has been a basic tenet of U.S. foreign policy and a basic security interest of the world at large ever since. The Reagan administration remains firmly committed to the goal of preventing the spread of nuclear weapons. Such proliferation could trigger new and grave dangers for America's security and well-being and indeed for that of all the world's peoples. Desperate leaders in future high-stakes conflicts might not shrink from nuclear blackmail or even from the use of nuclear weapons if they were available. A conventional clash between nuclear-armed states in a conflict-prone region might escalate by accident or miscalculation to a local nuclear exchange. It cannot be discounted that such a nuclear clash might threaten to involve the superpowers themselves. With proliferation, also, terrorist groups could more easily acquire nuclear weapons to extort concessions.

Preventing the spread of nuclear weapons, then, is not solely of interest to the superpowers: it is vital to all countries and regions. The security of the countries in those regions to which nuclear weapons might spread would be most immediately and seriously affected. By their adherence to the NPT, more than 100 countries have recognized this fact.

The NPT is the cornerstone of the global effort to realize the benefits of the peaceful use of nuclear energy while guarding against its misuse. The United States is committed to encouraging the use of nuclear energy for peaceful ends. President Reagan's October 1981 policy statement on nuclear power stressed that his administration will foster increased domestic reliance on nuclear power but will not compromise public health and safety. The Reagan

7

administration has sought both to streamline the licensing process and to remove regulatory impediments that have contributed to the utilities' reluctance to purchase new nuclear power plants. The embargo on domestic reprocessing has been lifted, and private-sector involvement has been encouraged. Demonstration of breeder-reactor technology is moving ahead. In the closing days of the Ninety-seventh Congress, long-sought legislation to create operational facilities for handling high-level nuclear waste was enacted.

Many other nations are likewise committed to meeting an important part of their energy requirements through nuclear energy. The countries of EURATOM (European Atomic Energy Commission) and Japan already have advanced peaceful nuclear programs and many of them rely on nuclear power for a significant portion of their electricity; they are moving toward implementation of the breeder reactor. South Korea and Taiwan are developing increasingly sophisticated nuclear energy infrastructures; China, Egypt, and the Philippines are entering the nuclear energy world; and, closer to home, nuclear power is an important part of the Canadian, Mexican, Argentine, and Brazilian energy programs.

It is essential that the American nuclear industry play a role in this global nuclear energy future, just as it contributed to the initial development and worldwide implementation of nuclear power. It can be argued that this is necessary because of the economic and technical benefits of maintaining a sound nuclear industry. Contributions to a healthy balance of payments, more jobs, and tax revenues are at stake. But the strong nonproliferation and security benefits flowing from such a role may be even more important.

Because the United States has been a leading supplier of nuclear equipment and technology, it has been able to take the lead in the global nonproliferation effort. It was instrumental in creating the International Atomic Energy Agency (IAEA) in 1957, in launching the international safeguards system, and in securing agreement to the London Nuclear Suppliers' Group guidelines. As a major supplier, the United States plays a vital role in current efforts to strengthen the London guidelines. Its help is also important in shaping the deliberations on assurances of supply and on international plutonium storage now being conducted under IAEA auspices.

An End to Unilateralism

As we look to the decade ahead, in which the introduction of nuclear power into new countries and regions may be expected, our direct involvement and participation becomes even more important. For if the United States should fail to maintain its position as a leading nuclear exporter, other views on nonproliferation and safeguards would carry increasing weight in shaping global norms and practices; it is by no means certain that those views will be as strong and consistent as our own.

The Reagan administration will continue its efforts to remove impediments to the U.S. nuclear industry's desire to compete on a fair and equal basis with the nuclear industries of other supplier countries. The United States stands ready to cooperate with friendly countries, contributing technology, materials, and know-how in programs appropriate to the evolving energy requirements and capabilities of those countries. But, as its actions have demonstrated, the present administration has no intention of diluting its commitment to nuclear nonproliferation in pursuit of commercial gain.

Over the past two years, changes in the nonproliferation policy of the United States have been evident. Previously, that policy relied heavily on a strategy of technology denial—a strategy based on the near-theological notion that the very use of nuclear power was the driving force behind proliferation. But denial has not worked. Indeed, Gerard Smith and George Rathjens wrote in *Foreign Affairs*, that the policy initiatives of recent years and the NNPA [Nuclear Nonproliferation Act] have had little relevance to real proliferation problems. To deal with those problems, what is needed now is not abstract debate about nuclear power, but nuclear common sense.

"Common sense" simply means seeing the world as it is, not as we might wish it to be. If we look at the problem in this way, it seems clear that the United States should base its nuclear nonproliferation policy on the fact that America no longer has the dominant influence in the nuclear field—whether scientific or commercial—that it once enjoyed. As mastery of the technology has become more widespread, the ability of the United States to persuade others to follow its lead (let alone to dictate their nuclear energy choices) has diminished.

We must turn away from the unilateral approach that has characterized dealings with our nuclear partners and emphasize instead a cooperative approach, working together to reach agreement on how nuclear relations are to be conducted. A continuation of unilateralism will certainly not help to achieve our nonproliferation goals; it could even sour our international relationships beyond the nuclear sphere. Only through a cooperative approach can we expect to develop the institutions, codes of conduct, and practices that go to make up a sound nonproliferation regime.

If we are to look at the world as it really is, we must be ready to treat different things differently, to make legitimate distinctions. In the past, there was a tendency to lump all countries together and to treat them all alike in an unrealistic, even patronizing, manner. This led to rancorous and counterproductive disputes with the EURATOM countries and Japan. Yet, both EURATOM and Japan have unimpeachable nonproliferation credentials.

Japan and EURATOM recognize the need for restraint in exporting sensitive items; they have supported efforts to develop international safeguards; they have cooperated on other nonproliferation initiatives. Moreover, neither Japan nor any of the non-nuclear-weapon states in EURATOM intends to develop nuclear weapons. These realities must be reflected in America's nuclear cooperation with those countries, and their long-term nuclear energy needs must be taken into account.

Common sense also suggests that the level to which a country's nuclear power program has developed may be an important ingredient in defining the nature of our nuclear relations with that country. President Reagan has said that the United States will not inhibit civil reprocessing and breeder programs in countries having advanced nuclear programs, so long as such activities do not constitute a proliferation risk. Yet, it is desirable to avoid premature commitment to reprocessing or breeder-reactor activity in countries whose nuclear programs are less-sophisticated. We shall not dictate the nuclear energy programs of other countries, but neither shall we encourage advanced fuel-cycle activities unless they are warranted as a coherent part of an advanced nuclear program.

No one denies that plutonium is a dangerous substance and one that must be carefully controlled. But to deal with the world as it is, we must first acknowledge that plutonium is and will continue to be used as a nuclear fuel, even if the extent of that use remains uncertain. In EURATOM and Japan, plutonium fuel is believed by many to be more economical and needed sooner than may be the case in the United States. Breeder-reactor development, for example, is well advanced in France and continues to move forward in Japan. The United Kingdom continues its research, and the decision of German utilities to defray 20 percent of the cost of completing the Kalkar demonstration breeder signals their desire to keep all options open.

Rather than engaging EURATOM and Japan in "theological" discussions about the desirability of a so-called plutonium economy, we are working seriously with them to find the safest way to undertake reprocessing and to use plutonium. Together we must design rigorous safeguards for such advanced nuclear activities. We must also try to restrict actual reprocessing and other fuel-cycle facilities to as few sites as possible and be prepared to deal with problems of security, transportation, and waste disposal. Cooperation in each of these areas is essential, and cooperation will not be fostered by talk of suspending nuclear exports to our friends and allies.

Treat Causes, Not Symptoms

If we are to be guided by common sense, we must concentrate on the underlying causes of a problem, not on its surface symptoms. Too often in the recent past, however, U.S. policy has focused on the symptomatic aspects of proliferation. Denial of technological help—in the mistaken belief that such denial would guarantee that nuclear explosives could not be developed—was the centerpiece of U.S. policy. As we have seen, denial is simply not enough: a sound strategy should address the motivations that might lead a nation toward the development of nuclear explosives. It is clear that understanding those motivations, rather than focusing on technological capabilities alone, is a key to successful long-term nonproliferation efforts.

There are, for example, a number of highly developed industrial nations that, if they thought their national-security interests demanded it, could quickly produce nuclear explosive devices. The fact that they have not done so has little or nothing to do with their technological capabilities. Rather, it reflects the structure and content of their security relationships and the general political climate shaping their policies.

This is not to say that there is no situation in which a strategy of technology denial is called for or that denial can never succeed. Measures to delay the development of the technical means of acquiring nuclear weapons are a necessary part of U.S. nonproliferation policy. President Reagan has made it abundantly clear that the United States will strive to inhibit the spread of sensitive technology, facilities, and material, particularly where the danger of proliferation exists. Nonetheless, a sound approach cannot rely on a strategy of denial and have any assurance of long-term success. Such a policy can buy time— perhaps, in some cases, substantial time—but that time must be used wisely. New initiatives must be pursued in order to reduce the underlying motivations that might lead a country to seek nuclear weapons.

Steps to alleviate military and political insecurity are an important part of the effort to reduce the motivation to "go nuclear." The United States is taking such steps. Throughout the postwar period, strong and credible U.S. alliances have been crucial to the realization of our nonproliferation objectives. Equally important are diplomatic initiatives to minimize regional instability.

Ways must also be found to dampen the suspicions potential rivals may have about each other's longer-term nuclear intentions. Implementation of the Treaty of Tlatelolco in Latin America would contribute to that goal, and the Reagan administration has succeeded in getting Senate approval of Protocol I to that treaty. It is to be hoped that those countries in Latin America which have not yet accepted the treaty will see fit to do so, both in their own interest and in their neighbors'. Adherence to the Nonproliferation Treaty, too, can be a big step toward reducing mutual suspicion, and the United States takes every opportunity to win new adherents to the NPT. Egypt's accession in 1981 was another milestone on that road.

By accepting safeguards on all its nuclear activities, a nation gives concrete expression to its good intentions. In the view of IAEA Director-General Blix, IAEA safeguards are measures through which states, in the exercise of their sovereign will, rely upon an international organization to confirm through inspection that their actions conform to their stated intention not to acquire nuclear weapons. According to Blix the verification procedures should not be cosmetic but convincing. When assessing the effectiveness of these safe-guards, however, common sense dictates that we be wary of the trap of letting the best become the enemy of the good. The ongoing debate about the effec-tiveness of IAEA safeguards is a dramatic example of this syndrome. The problems confronting the agency, of course, must be squarely faced. Despite steady improvements over the past several years, the capabilities of the IAEA can still be enhanced.

More and better-trained inspectors as well as wider use of more-advanced safeguards equipment are needed. Further improvements in the IAEA's inter-nal management will yield greater effectiveness. In addition, the agency needs to find ways of streamlining its internal lines of communication as well as better ways of communicating with the world at large. The United States is pursuing measures that should be helpful; in our efforts to improve, however, we must avoid exaggerating the agency's weaknesses. The IAEA's overall performance has been good and is getting better.

There must be a much clearer understanding of what the safeguards job en-tails. The agency's safeguards system is designed to detect and thus deter di-version of nuclear materials, not to prevent it. The IAEA is not a nuclear policeman. As we seek to make the agency an ever more effective institution, it is important not to forget that its credibility in the eyes of the world's nations is the essential ingredient for success. Repeated rehashing of old or alleged failings, without fair recognition of the vigorous efforts being made to over-come them, can damage that credibility.

As we ponder how to improve the vital safeguards role of the IAEA, we must never overlook its special character. Many member states have delegated considerable sovereign authority to the IAEA, making it unique among UN agencies. Alternative arrangements, if they could be forged at all, might be far less adequate.

The United States is ready to work with other countries to ensure that the IAEA remains a strong institution and that it is able to serve the legitimate needs of all its member states. Together we can rededicate the agency to the pursuit of its founding principles. The self-interest and common sense of all nations demands no less. Without an effective IAEA, the international non-proliferation effort would be critically weakened.

The Essence of Nuclear Common Sense

Some have suggested that we must begin now to think about how to live in a world covered with nuclear-weapons-toting nations. Such proliferation is inevitable, they say. Other commentators even go so far as to argue that the spread of nuclear weapons would not be so bad. As Kenneth Waltz put it in a publication of the International Institute of Strategic Studies, "more may be better." These views do not meet the test of common sense.

It simply is not true that widespread proliferation is inevitable: if we act decisively and promptly, much can be done to prevent it. It is useful to recall that in the early 1960s many responsible government officials predicted a world of 25 to 30 nuclear-weapon states by the 1980s. The adherence of some 120 non-nuclear-weapon states to the NPT is another major accomplishment—far beyond most predictions. There is reason to hope, then, that the future will not be so bleak. The notion that more proliferation may be better is equally false. Proliferation can only increase global instability and adversely affect the interests and well-being of all. It would threaten international order as we have known it and could lead to the breakdown of the nuclear peace we have enjoyed thus far—a breakdown that could occur not only by choice, but also by accident or miscalculation.

Since the first nuclear chain reaction more than forty years ago, the world has confronted both the promise and the threat of the atom. The promise is great, but so is the threat. The Reagan administration is committed to realizing the promise and controlling the threat. But success requires a restored spirit of cooperation—within the government, between industry and government, and among governments. Not least, we need a greater measure of nuclear common sense.

2

The Pendulum Swings,
While the Clock Ticks

Lawrence Scheinman

Avoidance of the spread of nuclear weapons has occupied a central role in U.S. strategic and foreign policy since the dawn of the atomic age. Nuclear weapons proliferation has been viewed as incompatible with U.S. security interests, and with the goal of maintaining a stable and peaceful world order. It has been regarded as a threat to alliance cohesion and credibility; as a potential source for the enlargement and intensification of local and regional conflict; and as a generally complicating factor in the management of international politics.

On balance, relatively few U.S. policy objectives have enjoyed the same degree of continuity and consistent bipartisan support as nonproliferation. U.S. nonproliferation policy has evolved through several phases during the past several decades with virtually no dissent on the objective from any segment of the policy community and, to the extent that it has focused on proliferation-related issues, with the general approval of public opinion. Where differences have arisen, they have involved tactics for achieving mutually agreed ends.

Three major phases can be identified: the period of secrecy (1946-54); the Atoms for Peace era (1954-74); and the post–Atoms for Peace era, in which we still find ourselves today and for which a terminal point is difficult to predict. Shifts from one phase to the next are the consequence of complex considerations, including assessments of the effectiveness of existing policies in achieving specified objectives; technology development that opens to consideration new economic, technical, or political opportunities not previously available; commercial considerations; and changes in the general and specific environments in which nuclear technology is located. Real and perceived changes in energy supply and demand, and assessments of the attractiveness of energy alternatives (including advanced technologies involving nuclear energy) are examples of what may fall within the framework of environmental change. The emergence of new states from colonialism, imbued with strong beliefs about the relationship of control over high technologies to modernization, economic development, and manifest sovereignty, is another example. These considerations—individually and collectively, at times mutually reinforcing and at times in contradiction to one another—play powerful shaping roles in the dynamics of nonproliferation.

It is important to understand that nonproliferation policy has always contained elements of both control and denial, with greater or lesser emphasis on one or the other depending upon the political circumstances of the time. The era of secrecy and denial contained some cooperative elements, and the era of Atoms for Peace embodied certain constraints and limitations on sharing nuclear technology. The key features of the latter era included elements of *cooperation* (the Geneva Conferences on Peaceful Uses of Atomic Energy, the International Atomic Energy Agency, and bilateral agreements for cooperation); *control* (the principle of international safeguards on cooperative transactions to verify adherence by recipients to their undertakings and commitments to use assistance for peaceful purposes only); and *denial* (the Nonproliferation Treaty undertaking not to develop or acquire nulcear explosives or to assist others in so doing). Control and denial are also central features of the post-Atoms for Peace era, although they appear to be less stable, more frequently revised, and less universally supported than in the past. Looked at over time, nonproliferation policy gives the appearance of a pendulum swinging ponderously from denial toward controlled cooperation and back again toward a more denial-oriented approach. This is not an unreasonable perspective, but it is incomplete. As the pendulum has swung, time and the political environment in which cooperation, control, and denial are practiced have changed. This makes earlier policies less easy to pursue and the need for newer, adaptive measures more evident.

Controlled Nuclear Cooperation

From the time that the pendulum swung from secrecy and denial to the controlled cooperation of Atoms for Peace, a regime of principles, rules, institutions, and processes relating to nonproliferation has evolved. While our main concern here is the current transitional period that began in 1974, it is useful to recall briefly some of the main features of the regime that had developed to that point.[1] Institutionally, three features bear emphasis: (1) a network of bilateral agreements, which implemented international nuclear cooperation and trade, and contained commitments by recipients to refrain from misappropriating the assistance provided for peaceful purposes and to accept supplier inspections to ensure that those commitments were being met; (2) the establishment of the International Atomic Energy Agency (IAEA) to facilitate and promote the peaceful uses of nuclear energy and eventually to absorb responsibility for implementing safeguards to verify not only bilateral undertakings but also voluntary commitments assumed under the Nonproliferation Treaty (NPT) and the Treaty of Tlatelolco; and (3) the Nonproliferation Treaty itself, which symbolized the norm of nonproliferation and created an international framework within which nuclear cooperation and development could proceed in a manner supportive of national and international security.

Expectations also developed within the framework of proliferation constraints. Advanced industrial states looked to unimpeded development of peaceful uses of nuclear energy and to the opportunity to compete in the marketplace for nuclear clients. And, developing countries sought assured access to nuclear materials and technologies that were widely perceived as central to plans for economic modernization and industrialization. Conventional wisdom emerged on fuel-cycle development, particularly on reprocessing and plutonium use. It was assumed that at a certain threshold point in power reactor development, reprocessing would become appropriate and, in light of a presumed limitation on accessible and economic uranium resources, necessary. U.S. bilateral agreements were written with this possibility in mind and, in the early 1970s, the Atomic Energy Commission began writing enrichment service contracts whose fulfillment was conditional on reprocessing of spent nuclear fuel. The IAEA statute provided an agency right of approval of the *means* of reprocessing of material over which it had jurisdiction, and for requiring deposit of excess plutonium stocks with the agency. While this confirmed expectations all around about the eventual emergence of plutonium as an important and increasingly routine factor in the nuclear energy economy, the special provisions surrounding plutonium and the restraint exercised in sharing sensitive fuel-cycle technology underscored its special nature and need for singular treatment.

Overall, from the mid-1950s to the mid-1970s, there was widespread consensus on the basic acceptability of a policy of controlled nuclear cooperation and on its main features. Reliance on external sources for supply of equipment and material under conditions that limited and restrained certain conduct was not seen as incompatible with the exercise of sovereignty. Many states saw the commitment not to develop or acquire nuclear weapons in exchange for peaceful nuclear cooperation as compatible with their sovereign status. These states understood those commitments and the associated verification safeguards as contributing to their own national security by reducing suspicions about their own nuclear intent, thereby removing possible incentives of their neighbors to themselves seek nuclear weapons. Regarding proliferation primarily as a political act and the consequence of conscious political decisions, many were prepared to put their faith in the ability of the regime as then formed to contain proliferation. In the early 1970s, the entire array of bilateral agreements, nonproliferation undertakings, international (and increasingly comprehensive) safeguards, and the cautious approach of supplier states to the transfer of sensitive technologies appeared to most to be in acceptable balance. The pendulum had come to rest at the point of controlled nuclear cooperation with primary emphasis on international safeguards to verify national nonproliferation undertakings and commitments.[2]

Changing Perspectives and Policies

The year 1974 was a watershed year. Three factors converged to raise concern about the adequacy of the nonproliferation regime and to undermine the prevailing consensus in its ability to contain proliferation. One was the oil crisis, which stimulated greater interest in nuclear energy, particularly insofar as it would help reduce external energy dependence. That invoked greater attention to plutonium recovery, thermal recycle, and breeder development. The second factor was India's detonation of a nuclear device, underscoring the potential for nonindustrial developing countries to exploit successfully the dark side of nuclear technology. The third, and most ominous, factor was the projected transfer of sensitive fuel-cycle technology and facilities to several countries with only incipient nuclear programs, three of which (South Korea, Taiwan, and Pakistan) were located in unstable regions and themselves either harbored or were the targets of revanchist sentiments.

This was a different pattern of technological dissemination than initially contemplated by the United States, and it was deemed to require some kind of response if further erosion of the status quo was to be avoided. Over the course of a several-year period spanning the Ford and Carter administrations, the United States launched a two-pronged approach aimed at reinforcing the nonproliferation regime and seeking to restore confidence in the concept of controlled nuclear cooperation. The approach drew a broad spectrum of reaction, and reveals a mixed record of success and failure. Some critics contended that reinforcement measures did not go far enough. Their views are reflected in the continuing efforts through Congress and public education to increase constraints on nuclear transactions and to narrow the definition of the scope of legitimate nuclear activity. Others argued that on balance the U.S. approach after 1976, when policies that will be discussed below were first invoked, diminished U.S. credibility with its traditional nuclear partners and resulted in alienation and distrust on the part of newer entrants into the nuclear energy arena. The latter views shape some of the contours of the Reagan administration concept of how to reestablish the United States as a global nuclear leader and as a reliable supplier and cooperating partner.

The first strand of reactive U.S. policy focused on export policy changes. It generated only modest differences with our traditional industrial partners, and established rules of the game that largely define the current boundaries of the nonproliferation regime. It involved the mobilization of the principals into the Nuclear Suppliers Group so as to reach agreement on the terms and conditions under which future nuclear exports would be made. Underlying this effort was a concern that in an increasingly competitive marketplace, suppliers might seek to capture markets by imposing fewer constraints. The Federal Republic of Germany's agreement with Brazil rightly or wrongly was construed in this manner.

The primary objective was to ensure that safeguards not become bargaining chips in commercial nuclear competition. The outcome preferred by the United States would have been a universal requirement of full-scope safeguards as a condition for any nuclear export. Although favored by a number of suppliers, and the condition effectively applied to all nonweapon NPT parties, this failed to win French and German support. The agreed guidelines only provided that any export of items on a comprehensive "trigger list" drawn up by the suppliers would have to be placed under international safeguards. The United States has persisted in its quest for supplier agreement on mandatory comprehensive safeguards and now appears to be closer to achieving success.

A second U.S. objective, which reflected diminished confidence in international safeguards, was the interposing of technological barriers to proliferation in the form of a suppliers' agreement not to undertake further transfers of reprocessing or enrichment technology. This was also rejected by a number of other suppliers as too sweeping a restriction and likely to generate drives for nuclear independence in a number of countries over whom no means of exercising influence would remain. It also was perceived as altering the definition of proliferation from the NPT criterion of acquiring nuclear explosive devices to acquiring *capabilities*, which, given relevant political decisions, could be appropriated to weapons purposes but were also consistent with peaceful nuclear development. Nevertheless, consensus was reached among the suppliers that restraint should be exercised with respect to the transfer of sensitive technology. France and the FRG, the two main potential suppliers of reprocessing technology, subsequently announced unilaterally that they did not intend further such transfers in the foreseeable future. Additionally, the eventually agreed guidelines contained an important provision adapted from the French and German agreements with Pakistan and Brazil, respectively: transferred technology itself would come under safeguards, and any similar facility constructed by the recipient within a designated period of time (twenty years) would be presumed to involve replicated technology and thus be obligatorily placed under international safeguards. The burden of proving otherwise would rest with the recipient.

These supplier guidelines induced lively discussions among the suppliers over preferred strategies for dealing with the reinforcement of nonproliferation. At issue was whether to rely on safeguards and national undertakings, or to develop additive restraints, such as technological denial or specially conditioned technology transfers. But differences did not cause any breaks in the supplier ranks; rather, they reflected a renewed and reinforced consensus on the terms and conditions of doing international nuclear business. Although not fully satisfactory, especially to those concerned about the general effectiveness of a regime largely dependent on national undertakings and international verification safeguards, the guidelines did reflect an elevated consensus.

The new emphasis on caution and restraint in the transfer of technology struck disproportionately at Third World nations. It was widely perceived among them as tantamount to deprivation of access to civil nuclear technology and full access to the peaceful benefits of atomic energy, and as an extension into the peaceful nuclear realm of the pattern of differentiated treatment between North and South, haves and have-nots, which they saw as dominating the international system. Third World states party to the NPT interpreted this as violative of its spirit and intent, and even the letter of Article IV of the treaty, which was seen as the quid pro quo for accepting verified international undertakings regarding nuclear behavior. As a consequence, perceptions of discrimination and neocolonialism, this time in the realm of high technology, were reinforced. These perceptions have led to severe criticism of the nuclear-weapon states in the review conferences of the treaty and underlie the Mexican-Yugoslavian initiative for the UN-sponsored Peaceful Uses of Nuclear Energy (PUNE) conference to be held in 1986.

The second strand of post-1974 U.S. nonproliferation policy, which involved reprocessing and plutonium use, took a rather different turn and became the source of considerable controversy between the United States and its industrial nuclear partners. It entailed a decision to reassess conventional fuel-cycle assumptions and the nuclear development strategy that had guided nuclear activity since the inception of the Atoms for Peace Program. This decision came in 1976, when nonproliferation policy and the adequacy of the prevailing nuclear regime had become an issue in the presidential campaign.

First, President Ford declared that the United States would no longer regard reprocessing and plutonium recycling as necessary and inevitable steps in the nuclear fuel cycle, and that the United States would defer such activities until it was clear that the world community could effectively overcome the associated risks of proliferation. Other states were invited to join in a three-year moratorium on the export of reprocessing facilities and technology. Then, President Carter announced a more far-reaching policy of indefinite deferral of reprocessing and recycling in the United States and a restructuring of the breeder program to ensure that whatever breeder was eventually brought to commercialization would not pose an undue threat to society. In neither case did the United States actually seek to impose similar policy on its cooperating partners, but it was clear that similar decisions would be welcomed and preferred.

There were, however, some obvious effects on cooperation. In the case of Japan, for example, the United States found it inexpedient to proceed with a joint safeguardability determination regarding a recently completed pilot reprocessing facility. This led to a series of interim arrangements allowing circumscribed operation of that plant for U.S.-origin fuel. With respect to the transfer of spent fuel to France and Great Britain for reprocessing, it seemed inconsistent with policy to endorse business as usual. This led to a limited case-by-case approach to reprocessing U.S.-origin fuel in those facilities. Additionally, Congress enacted legislation (the Nuclear Nonproliferation Act of 1978, NNPA) that imposed restrictions on the nuclear fuel-cycle programs of nations cooperating with the United States, and established several timetables and conditions against the better judgment of the administration.

The thrust of this second strand of policy directly affected nuclear development plans in the advanced nuclear states, many of whom had made large-scale commitments to a fuel-cycle development strategy that assumed an eventual move to plutonium as a fuel. They felt vulnerable because of their generally high degree of energy resource dependence. None relished the thought of having to face domestic opposition to nuclear power, which was fed by doubts expressed at the official level in the leading nuclear nation. In addition, some were frankly concerned that their nuclear industries might suffer as a consequence of the convergence of a restrained external market (due to the parameters established by the Nuclear Suppliers Group guidelines) and a diminished domestic market (due to the internal impact of policies projected from the United States). Some European critics regarded United States policy in this respect as shortsighted because excess pressure on their internal market could make it difficult, if not impossible, to adhere to external market restraint agreements.[3] From this perspective, U.S. nonproliferation interests would in their view best be served by reinforcing and facilitating the growth of domestic nuclear programs in the advanced industrial states rather than by forcing them to absorb both export and internal development restraints.

The Carter administration's legacy is less likely to be its interrogation of conventional assumptions and wisdom regarding the nuclear fuel cycle (which is shared with the Ford administration) than its initiation of the International Nuclear Fuel Cycle Evaluation (INFCE). INFCE's strength lay first in the processes it set in motion, including subsequently constituted committees to deal with assurance of supply, plutonium storage, and spent fuel management;

and second in its contribution to defusing what was a growing trend toward recrimination, confrontation, and polarization, and encouraging instead rational discussion.

It also yielded some substantive results. While views on the appropriateness of different fuel-cycle strategies did not change, most participants achieved a deeper appreciation of the proliferation risks associated with certain fuel-cycle activities; a sharpened sense of the need to take proliferation considerations into account in making fuel-cycle decisions and in deploying fuel-cycle facilities; and a clearer understanding of the measures required to reduce if not eliminate those risks. Perhaps more important, many countries emerged from the INFCE sensitized to the collective nature of responsibility for avoiding proliferation by whatever path. The problem was understood to be universally shared and not the special concern of the superpowers or a few other states. On the other hand, countries that originally held that the problem of proliferation was primarily a technical problem gained a greater sense of the limits of technical fixes, and came more fully to appreciate the political dimensions of the proliferation problem.

Current Policy

Two features of nonproliferation policy during the Carter presidency served as particular points of departure for revisiting basic assumptions by the present administration. One was the emphasis in the application of nonproliferation policy on avoiding discrimination to the extent possible, and on establishing and implementing a policy of universal, general applicability. Critics argued that historically weapons acquisition resulted not from abuse of peaceful activities but from dedicated military programs, and that the new policy gave disproportionate emphasis to the civilian fuel cycle as a path to proliferation. The other feature of Carter (and, even more, congressional) policy that invited criticism was its unilateralism, particularly the effort singularly to redefine the rules of the game and conditions for cooperation with respect to already existing agreements and undertakings with partners in good nonproliferation standing. The conversion of the policy goal of full-scope safeguards into a condition for issuing export licenses under existing agreements for cooperation was one example; the retroactive provisions in the NNPA, such as those requiring renegotiation of agreements to include prior consent rights over spent-fuel disposal as a condition of continued cooperation (subject to presidential waiver in specified circumstances), were another. Combined with the global and undifferentiated policy strategy described above, this approach worked to diminish confidence in the United States as a viable and dependable partner and reliable supplier.

Recognition of factors such as these had already stimulated some reassessment within the Carter administration regarding optimal paths for achieving U.S. nonproliferation objectives, and some modifications already were in train in the year before the presidential election. Additionally, policy implementation during the Carter years was always more moderate, flexible, and accommodating than the policy rhetoric or statutory language might have suggested. In pursuit of its effort to enhance the nonproliferation regime and to reconstitute a broad-based consensus on the parameters of legitimate and appropriate conduct, the Carter administration had in one way or another met many of the most serious concerns of its cooperating partners who were in good nonproliferation standing. But these were largely in the form of interim, temporary, and ad hoc adjustments, and left the basic policy—and even more important, the statutory provisions that set the policy boundaries—intact and hanging like the proverbial Damoclean sword over the head of the nuclear partners of the United States.

The Reagan administration took office committed to reestablishing the United States as a reliable nuclear supplier consistent with national nonproliferation goals. Proliferation is seen primarily as a political problem, and only secondarily as a technological issue involving only capabilities. Unmotivated to develop nuclear weapons, technologically capable states will, according to this approach, shun them. Japan, the Federal Republic of Germany, Sweden, and Switzerland are cited as cases in point. For these countries, the earlier conventional wisdom on fuel-cycle development, as modified by supplier agreements and evolving policies, should be reinstated. Where, on the other hand, these same conditions do not obtain, either because of national or regional instability, political uncertainties, nonproliferation doubts, or the like, a different, more circumspect and cautious approach should be adopted. However, to the extent that nuclear energy can offer greater energy abundance and energy security without at the same time posing an increased risk of proliferation or threat to international security, it should be made available. In either case, nonproliferation policy should be integrated with overall U.S. foreign policy and national security interests and not be treated as a free-standing policy objective. these considerations dictate the major elements of the approach to be followed: liberalization; differentiation and selectivity; vigilant attention to nonproliferation; and building bridges to supplier and recipient states alike. Effective implementation of these goals is seen as facilitating achievement of the overall objective of reinstating the United States in the front rank of nuclear development and as a reliable, predictable partner.

With respect to the element of trade liberalization, the administration is committed to increasing U.S. nuclear exports and reestablishing the United

States as a vigorous and competitive partner in international nuclear commerce. It holds that such policies can increase U.S. influence or leverage while increasing the health of the U.S. nuclear industry, an objective to which it is more committed than was its predecessor. The administration has not, as its critics have alleged, proposed to overturn all controls over and restrictions on U.S. nuclear exports and cooperation. It has stated that it will continue to adhere to past U.S. policy and practice, which restricts certain nuclear exports, and to apply the controls embodied in U.S. statutes. And, responding to critics who question how well proliferation will fare when these two values are juxtaposed, the administration has reaffirmed that nonproliferation objectives will not yield to commercial interests and has urged a similar commitment on the part of other suppliers.

The practical effect of this liberalization relates largely to reprocessing and plutonium-use policies, and the principal (but not exclusive) beneficiaries are intended to be Japan and the EURATOM states, which are energy deficient, sensitive to problems of energy security, and heavily committed to fuel-cycle strategies entailing plutonium use. Even with these countries, whose nonproliferation credentials are unimpeachable, however, establishing accommodative policies with respect to U.S.-origin fuel is intended to be predicated on achieving "satisfactory mutual understandings . . . on enhancing international cooperation to improve the non-proliferation regime and safeguards."[4] This policy remains unimplemented thus far due to unresolved differences between the United States and its industrial partners and between the administration and Congress. The failure to achieve rapid agreement despite the policy's more accommodating posture suggests the possible oversimplification of problems on the part of the incumbent critics of Carter policies, and puts the administration to the difficult test of achieving a reconciliation that truly preserves the underlying principles of nonproliferation.

The turn to differentiation and selectivity follows from rejection of the feasibility or utility of conducting a policy based on nondiscrimination when the interests, reliability, and levels of development of nations involved in nuclear activity are so disparate. The administration has, rather, chosen to treat nations differentially. That principle is inherent in the reprocessing and plutonium-use policies mentioned above, and is evident in the president's statement of 16 July 1981 that "the United States will continue to inhibit the transfer of sensitive nuclear materials, equipment and technology, particularly where the danger of proliferation demands."[5] Among the important remaining questions are whether differentiated treatment will induce even more comprehensive and coherent supplier state strategies, and how Third World countries might view and react to this in terms of the concept of reliable supply.

The importance of vigilant nonproliferation follows from current perceptions of proliferation risks. In a diminished market such as prevails today, the risks to the nonproliferation regime are greater as the economic health or even survival of some suppliers comes into play. This recognition, along with other considerations, has led the administration to place considerable emphasis on the importance of a strong nonproliferation regime. The presidential statement of July 1981 is unequivocal in this regard. It strongly reaffirms U.S. commitment to preventing the spread of nuclear weapons; supporting and reinforcing the NPT and Treaty of Tlatelolco; improving and enhancing the IAEA and international safeguards; and inhibiting the transfer of sensitive nuclear materials and technology where such transfers would increase the risk of proliferation. It calls for more effective supplier cooperation to combat proliferation risks, including taking action in response to violations of treaty obligations or international safeguards agreements. This statement of policy has been supported in active ways, including efforts to have all principal suppliers adopt comprehensive safeguards as a condition for significant new supply, and fostering the upgrading of the safeguards "trigger lists" as well as seeking supplier consensus on export control of dual-use items.

Very little, if any, of this approach is different from the actions or inclinations of previous administrations. The primary difference involves the emphasis on motivational considerations rather than capabilities, as well as on nuclear weapons acquisition rather than on the development of a nuclear industrial base. The difficult questions at this level relate to distinguishing where particular activities or events constitute a proliferation risk and where they do not. In shifting emphasis from capability to motivation, U.S. policy explicitly injects subjective judgment regarding the intentions of other nations. While perhaps more "realistic," this approach strings up a number of tightropes on which U.S. policymakers will have to perform some extraordinary balancing acts.

Finally, the efforts to build bridges are derived in part from critics of earlier nonproliferation policies, who questioned the wisdom of isolating the United States from key supplier states as well as from states reluctant to adhere to the NPT or to accept comprehensive safeguards, contending that isolation only diminishes the likelihood of curtailing the spread of nuclear weapons. Without dialogue and interaction there would be no opportunity to alter national views. Instead, bridge-building has been advocated, i.e. maintaining some level of dialogue and cooperation consistent with statutory limitations on international nuclear transactions. With respect to U.S. relations with the other principal suppliers, bridge-building appears to have had some beneficial results, including agreement among the Zangger Group members to include centrifuge enrichment components in the safeguards "trigger lists," as well as cooperation in planning for the 1985 NPT Review Conference and in maintaining the integrity of the IAEA in face of increasing political problems. Stabilization of relations among the Western states also has provided the United States with the opportunity to carry forward its case for universally agreed comprehensive safeguards, although success in that effort remains to be achieved. Critics, of course, would argue that a high price has been paid for simply keeping a constructive dialogue going insofar as one of the key concessions made by the administration relates to opening the door to a plutonium economy. Further, these critics would assert that it is unclear that more substantial gains in support of U.S.-preferred nonproliferation outcomes will ensue.

As for bridge-building to the hold-out states, the record is far less persuasive. Under this approach the United States has facilitated the fueling of South Africa's Koeberg reactors from French sources, the transfer of heavy water to Argentina from the FRG, the provision of enriched uranium fuel to Brazil from Western Europe, and the substitution of France for the United States as supplier of fuel for India's Tarapur reactors. One may reasonably ask, what have we received for these actions? While it is still too early to make definitive judgments, only one claim of "achievement" can thus far be made: South Africa's announcement that it would pursue the practice of the principal nuclear suppliers in requiring safeguards on its exports and that it would consider placing IAEA safeguards on its semicommercial enrichment facility. The latter point involves a resumption of earlier discussions rather than a "breakthrough" and, significantly, does not extend to Pretoria's pilot enrichment plant; the former point reflects a modest gain. On the other hand, neither South Africa nor the others have themselves taken steps toward accepting comprehensive safeguards or adhering to the NPT, or toward significantly closing down opportunities for states outside the nonproliferation regime to find alternate ways to circumvent supplier state controls. The bridges built thus far, while intended to provide for two-way traffic, appear to have been traveled in only one direction. This is not an argument for abandoning the bridge-building concept but for ensuring that it brings genuinely reciprocal nonproliferation benefit.

In general, one of the least satisfactory approaches to nonproliferation that the United States could take, now or in the wake of a change of administration, would be radical departure from prevailing policies. Such action could only produce more uncertainty and loss of confidence in the broader international arena. That is true were the nonproliferation pendulum to swing sharply in *either* direction: toward cooperative liberalization or toward restrictive denial. Where they are weak, our policies need to be shored up; where inadequate, they require additive support. In the long run, if we are to preserve and enhance the gains we have thus far made in achieving widespread commitment to the nonproliferation ethic, we must do so in a manner that builds confidence on the part of others regarding the steadiness of our objectives and the sensitivity and reasonableness of our course. Nothing can guarantee the continued integrity of the regime, but some strategies are surely to be preferred over others. In this case, we should seek to keep the pendulum in equilibrium.

Notes

1. See J.S. Nye, "Maintaining a Nonproliferation Regime," in *Nuclear Proliferation: Breaking the Chain*, ed. G. Quester (Madison: University of Wisconsin Press, 1981), pp. 15-38.
2. For a general overview supporting this evolution, see B. Goldschmidt, "A Historical Survey of Nonproliferation Policies," *International Security* (Summer 1977): 69-87.
3. See. e.g., Pierre Lellouche, "International Nuclear Politics," *Foreign Affairs* (Winter 1979).
4. Testimony of Deputy Secretary of Energy Kenneth Davis before the Subcommittee on Energy, Nuclear Proliferation and Government Processes, Senate Committee on Governmental Affairs, 9 September 1982.
5. Presidential statement on nonproliferation and peaceful nuclear cooperation policy, 16 July 1981.

3

Salvaging the Peaceful Atom

Henry David Sokolski

Over the past three years, when nuclear policy analysts have gathered, perhaps the two most-discussed questions have been how the Carter policies differ from those of Reagan and which of the two policies is sounder. Though I will also address these questions, I reject the assumption that differentiating between the two policies is the soundest way to judge their respective merits. Indeed, their key differences are best understood as variations on a shared belief in the underlying logic of Atoms for Peace. This common faith, in turn, is so basic to both policies and so defective that it more than overshadows whatever differences might exist between them. Unless the logic of Atoms for Peace is reformulated, neither policy can long succeed in meeting our national security requirements (by keeping the civilian atom peaceful) and at the same time promote civilian nuclear energy (or at least not hinder its businesslike development).

At first glance, Carter's policies do seem fundamentally different from those of the Reagan administration. Carter emphasized the need for tighter international controls and for reaching international consensus. Reagan, on the other hand, has emphasized bilateral cooperation and reliable supply. Yet, the net effect of both policies has been to promote looser nuclear controls. Thus, after sharing sensitive fuel-cycle technology through the International Nuclear Fuel Cycle Evaluation (to educate the world about the perils of plutonium), the Carter administration condoned breeder reactors and reprocessing for "advanced nations" (to stave off international popularization of thermal recycle) and tacitly approved international plutonium storage (to anticipate plutonium's widespread commercial use). Initially, the Carter justification in each of these cases was exceptional: the United States had to recognize the inevitable and get agreement where it could. What followed, though, were other nonproliferation imperatives that were no less controversial: the continued sale of nuclear fuel to India; the negotiation of reprocessing agreements with Japan; and the processing of nuclear-fuel retransfer requests without a clear showing of physical need. Finally, with Gerard Smith's suggested nonproliferation guidelines of 1980, each of these exceptions was reformulated and generalized into desirable rules.[1]

The Reagan administration has taken a somewhat different approach. Rather than trying to establish laws that would recommend withdrawal of nuclear support for suspect nations or emphasizing the need to secure more formal international horizontal-control agreements and greater safeguards, it has promoted nuclear trade as an essential means to moderate those nations whose nuclear irresponsibility is not yet patent (e.g., South Africa, Brazil, and—earlier—Argentina). If items licensed by the Nuclear Regulatory Commission cannot be exported directly to such nations, dual-purpose items can and are being exported. For nations having acceptable credentials, more substantial exports have been suggested. Perhaps export of light-water reactors and reactor components to Beijing (previously prohibited on the grounds that such exports might give the Chinese naval-reactor technology) could be accomplished. With the collapse of the near-term nuclear reactor export market, other sales—reprocessing technology to Japan (later perhaps to South Korea) and enrichment technology to Australia—have been considered.

At the same time, the administration has defended International Atomic Energy Agency (IAEA) safeguards, if not the agency itself. The IAEA's critics, argue the State Department and the Department of Energy, are wrong. IAEA safeguards have their faults but, in time, can be improved to meet current obligations. Fairly effective safeguards for reprocessing and enrichment, they argue, can be achieved. Indeed, helping to set such safeguard standards and establishing our world leadership are reasons to encourage the very commercialization projects—the Clinch River breeder reactor and the reprocessing facility at Barnwell—that Carter and Ford previously opposed because they were too dangerous to warrant the inherent safeguard risks.[2]

Certainly the Reagan administration has retreated from some of its bolder (and more politically costly) nuclear policy initiatives of 1981 and 1982. It has pulled back from efforts to process spent commercial fuel for weapons purposes. It is no longer trying publicly to persuade Argentina to sign the NPT (Nonproliferation Treaty) by approving dual-purpose nuclear exports. And, after public outcry, the administration prevented the export of helium 3 and a hot isostatic press to South Africa. Finally, Secretary of State Shultz has stated that stopping nuclear proliferation was one of his top priorities, and the administration *has* tightened several formal procedures concerning nuclear export controls.

The key point is that both in the Reagan and the Carter policies, the natural

tendency and result has been to move toward a *looser* understanding of nuclear controls. This shared tendency, moreover, is not accidental. Both administrations share in a broader policy—Atoms for Peace—which has always
tried to promote U.S. nuclear exports, as an aid to building a domestic U.S.
nuclear industry, and encouraged multilateral and bilateral nuclear understanding conducive to horizontal arms control.[3] Since the Eisenhower administration put forward the Atoms for Peace policy, pursuit of these two general
objectives has been the rule.

Different administrations may have differed over which of these two Atoms
for Peace objectives should be emphasized, but the net effects on nuclear export control of emphasizing one or the other have been disturbingly similar.
Thus, when presidents have emphasized nuclear trade, U.S. nuclear export
policy has required controls—but only just enough to make commercial activity respectable. When they have sought international agreement on civilian
nuclear controls, on the other hand, such a premium is placed on promoting
international concord that important nuclear control provisions are frequently
jettisoned for fear that their provocative character might upset the progress of
negotiations.

Keeping the Faith

This brings us to perhaps the most crucial similarity between the Reagan
and the Carter policies. As policies tied to the original objectives of Atoms for
Peace, neither has had any clear or direct connection to U.S. national security
objectives. Again, the twin assumption behind the Carter-Reagan efforts is
that sharing the peaceful atom provides nonproliferation leverage abroad and
that promoting a consensus on horizontal arms control makes the world a safer
place. The goal of U.S. national security is given lip service here. But nuclear
sales (''leverage'') or promoting nuclear concord (getting as many divergent
nations as possible to agree that *something* nuclear ought to be avoided) are
assumed to be necessary and sufficient means to national security. To keep
the atom peaceful; to keep nuclear trade respectable; to force nuclearly active
nations into at least talking about the desirability of keeping nuclear energy's
applications civilian—in short, to maintain the faith—that is the key.

Keeping this faith, however, often comes at a cost to our national security.
Again, appearances—*some* evidence of nations' increased desire to avoid nuclear weapons deployment—are important. This is so much so that embarrassing evidence (that which upsets appearances but which is essential to an appreciation of nuclear proliferation's national security implications) is selectively suppressed. Thus, flashes in the South Atlantic, which clearly suggested that a nuclear device had been tested, were dismissed (this, just before
the NPT international review meeting). Similarly, when the U.S. State De-

partment was attempting to have the French assume U.S. nuclear fuel commitments to India, officials publicly dismissed the probability that the Indians would reprocess spent fuel for weapons use (French safeguards presumably would prevent this). Yet, privately, this probability was offered as an argument in favor of transferring our fuel commitments to the French. Better that the Indians should reprocess weapons-usable plutonium under French supply than allow India to violate U.S. law under U.S. commitments.

Given the faint connection of the Carter-Reagan policies to U.S. national security (the key objective of Atoms for Peace, after all, is to encourage international nuclear consensus through technology transfers and negotiations), actions too often are taken with little or no regard for their full implications. It was only a year after the United States persuaded the South Koreans to call off a clandestine nuclear weapons program (Korean fears of a U.S. military withdrawal, we insisted, were unwarranted) that the Carter administration announced U.S. troops would be withdrawn (this to shore up human rights?). Similarly, it was only *after* Congress protested that the security implications of either the transshipment of reprocessed fuel of U.S. origin to Japan (100 kilograms of weapons-usable plutonium without any military escort) or of sensitive, nuclear-related sales to South Africa were examined closely. Of course, some attention has been paid to the defense implications of proliferation. But, national security casualness in the nuclear energy field has been the rule. Unfortunately, it has worsened with the spread of nuclear capabilities and with the increase in problem nations' nuclear competence. Indeed, as the prospect of nuclear proliferation has increased, so too has acceptance of the view that not only can nothing much be done, but that things are hardly as bad as some say. The original hope of Atoms for Peace—that nuclear openness and negotiation might at least establish a binding international presumption against nations acquiring nuclear weapons—has ironically become attractive to some only because it is one of the few easy and positive courses left.

How long can such thinking guide U.S. civilian nuclear policy? Much depends on politics and on the pace of nuclear weapons proliferation itself. The underlying logic of the Carter and Reagan policies—increase nuclear supply flexibility in the name of leverage and, at the same time, try to establish an international standard of nuclear restraint while avoiding diplomatic friction or confrontation with any but the smallest nation—suggests that logic's fragility. External events, such as a series of countries "going nuclear" in the 1990s, could bring down the whole structure. Israel and South Africa may well be followed by Pakistan, Iraq, South Africa, Taiwan, Argentina, or Brazil. With increased safeguard commitments, IAEA inspection failures are more likely to increase.

Also, there is always the threat of smaller events. What might the United States do if the Soviets were to allow or help Cuba to catch up with Argentina and Brazil? (Moscow has already announced that it will be too "difficult" to take back spent fuel from the reactor it will build in Cuba.) What might be NATO's response (particularly the Italian reaction) to news that the Soviets were actually building a reactor for Libya (a former Italian colony) and would allow Libya to keep the spent fuel?[4]

These are some of the difficulties a continued policy of Atoms for Peace might face from abroad. For the moment, though, the chief threat to the policy's continued vitality is its domestic politicization. Carter, in 1976, was first to use nuclear proliferation as a campaign issue, and he used it to distinguish himself from Reagan in 1980. Reagan, in turn, initially emphasized how different his nuclear nonproliferation policy would be from Carter's. Indeed, many liberals believe the Reagan administration is simply a pawn of the atomic industry and will only act responsibly concerning nuclear proliferation and nuclear export controls when badgered by the liberal press. Aggravating this impression are neoliberal efforts to capture the nuclear proliferation issue for national political consumption and the Democratic party's use of this issue in its arms control critique of Reagan. These moves, when combined with the recent efforts by environmental groups (who have long been concerned about proliferation) to tailgate the nuclear freeze and disarmament movements, might heighten the hawks' suspicions of those who focus on the nuclear proliferation problem.

Pronuclear Republicans and conservative Democrats, on the other hand, are only likely to antagonize these liberal critics. For pronuclear Republicans and conservative Democrats, controlling nuclear exports to date has had as much appeal as trying to control handguns. Such efforts have the disadvantage of constituting interference with the free market and large private investments. As a result, many of these people ironically have been willing to support the nuclear industry (to compensate for its overregulation) to the point of subsidizing large commercialization efforts. Meanwhile, nuclear proponents continue to urge their Democratic and Republican political friends to subsidize or support development of sensitive fuel-cycle activities (such as reprocessing and enrichment technology) and export of nuclear power plants to capital-scarce nations.

In response, liberal champions of stopping nuclear proliferation have already toyed with the idea of establishing a U.S. or nuclear-supplier-group moratorium on nuclear trade or at least on commercialized reprocessing. Unlikely of achieving success here, these liberals may well settle on an isolationist position of simply getting the United States out of the nuclear export business, "sensitive" nuclear sales being the first to go.

Perhaps the only variant in such liberal-conservative/pronuclear-antinuclear posturing has been an effort by fiscal conservatives over the past two years to challenge the utility of federal subsidies to the nuclear industry (such as the federal limit on nuclear companies' insurance liabilities, Export-Import Bank loans to the large nuclear vendors, and such economically dubious Department of Energy projects as the Clinch River breeder reactor and the gas centrifuge enrichment facility). This variant, though, hardly lends support to the subsidizing assumptions intrinsic to Atoms for Peace.

Indeed, none of the positions now being politically promoted in the United States is going to boost a continuation of current Atoms for Peace policy, and, even under the best conditions, that policy's vitality seems limited. We may continue to criticize sensitive exports to "irresponsible" nations (when embarassed into doing so) but end up over time simply expanding the number of "responsible" nations (for if a nation already has a weapons capability or is willing to negotiate toward even weak safeguards improvements, it is our duty to continue nuclear trade) and adding to the types of activities that are considered "safe" (for in the name of establishing new levels of international understanding, all things are possible). Again, such loosening of nuclear controls is inherent to the tension and focus of the Atoms for Peace objectives: to promote civilian nuclear energy while establishing an international consensus on horizontal arms control.

Now or Never

Can the United States continue to promote nuclear power and, at the same time, keep the atom peaceful? Yes, but only if the current logic of Atoms for Peace is replaced by one that is focused primarily on keeping the atom peaceful. Not only will the goal of promoting nuclear exports have to be made subservient to what is *economically* sound here and now, but nuclear negotiations will have to be made subservient to the task of promoting the long-term security of the United States and its allies.

In theory, the first transformation is possible. The export of nuclear technology can be profitable in a big way only if there is a large enough domestic market for the product—there must be sufficient demand to establish a significant difference between the product's average and marginal production costs. If construction of reprocessing and enrichment facilities cannot attract private support in this country, it hardly makes much long-term economic sense to try to promote domestic nuclear energy by selling such technology abroad. Similarly, nuclear activity that can survive commercially only with the help of substantial government subsidies ought not to be attempted in the first place. (I have in mind premature commercial-scale breeders and reprocessing plants as well as additional high-capital-cost enrichment capacity that private industry is unwilling to finance.) Not only are such ventures financially senseless in the United States, they also jeopardize significant long-term employment opportunities in the more-planned economies of our allies.

On the other hand, we ought not block by unwise regulation nuclear activities that could be both profitable and reasonably safe. Currently, in the United States and other nations having planned economies, the sole advantage of nuclear power—its low fuel-cycle costs relative to coal- or oil-fired generators—is simply passed through to the consumer. Few, if any, nuclear fuel economies are captured by the investor. In the United States, moreover, profits that might be gained from wheeling this low-cost power into regions served by other utilities now must be shared. If electricity generation were deregulated in the states so that these economies could be captured in the form of profits, then nuclear power would surely have a healthier future than it now faces. Eventually, the need for new and replacement generation will increase; coal plant costs are increasing; and the last nuclear power construction project to come on line in the United States—St. Lucie 2—was completed in about six years, for less than $1.5 billion, and met all Nuclear Regulatory Commission requirements.

Also, interim and long-term geological storage of foreign spent fuel could seriously undercut the international demand for reprocessing and could bring in significant revenue now. (Environmentalists might be enlisted to back the establishment of a surface repository, in exchange for an industry pledge not to reprocess until the fuel value recovered was sufficient to attract private financial support.) Improved light-water reactors and high-burnup fuels could save U.S. electricity buyers billions of dollars by the year 2000, reduce uranium and enrichment requirements, promote U.S. reactor sales, and make it easier to place safeguards on increased nuclear generation overseas.[5]

None of these steps requires massive government spending or dubious supplier-group exports to potential problem countries. Indeed, since the largest long-term market for nuclear electricity exists within the supplier-group nations (the Organization for Economic Cooperation and Development), it would be more natural to encourage substantial market sharing among those nations and use interdependence to curb the sort of nuclear commerce that gave Pakistan and Iraq their nuclear hardware. The French want to sell us cheap enrichment; other countries want to sell us cheap yellowcake; we have light-water technology that the British and Japanese want. A consumers' group *could* be established.

Beyond such reliance on the invisible hand, a truly sound nuclear power policy requires that we move beyond the Atoms for Peace preoccupation with trying to maintain or establish some sort of international consensus on nuclear power—even if that agreement is so watered down that it is not worth having. The presumed aim, after all, is to enhance international security, which in turn is supposed to enhance *our* security.

If we are to keep the atom peaceful, we must focus first on what U.S. national security requires. We must understand that the national security threats implicit to nuclear proliferation in Latin America, the Middle East, the Far East, and South Asia are quite real. Unless we begin to deal with these threats as if they are more significant than mere arms control or trade matters, our military, which we are so desperately trying to modernize for the year 2000, will find itself seriously restricted at the very time modernization is complete.

Nor should we assume that such restriction will come from dramatic events, such as a Libyan nuclear attack. More mundane events—such as the quiet acquisition of a significant nuclear force by a problem nation—can also cause serious military-diplomatic setbacks. Consider: U.S. military planning now assumes that we may have to project forces into the Persian Gulf region before the year 2010. How credible would be U.S. efforts to protect the gulf's oil fields or ports, however, if two or more local states had their own nuclear weapons? Would the gulf states be more willing to allow U.S. or NATO bases in the region (bases that are essential if the United States is to have any hope of deterring further Soviet incursion)? Would such proliferation make these bases easier to defend? Would it reduce the attractiveness of Soviet security guarantees to nonnuclear nations in the region?

Much still depends on what we do. Several steps have already been suggested. Other factors—our independent intelligence capabilities, our ability to protect allies militarily, our willingness to wrangle with nuclear-supplier allies over dangerous nuclear exports, and our skill in bureaucratically rewarding those who are proficient at executing our nuclear export policy—are also important. Indeed, unless strong measures are taken now, when the number of problem countries and nuclear exporters is tolerably low, we will find ourselves without effective means later, when the numbers are unmanageable. At that point, Atoms for Peace will die not only as a hope, but as a reality as well.[6]

Notes

1. Luther J. Carter, "Relaxation Seen in Nonproliferation Policy," *Science* (5 October 1979): 33.
2. See Joseph Pilat and Warren Donnelly, *The Reagan Administration Policy for Preventing the Further Spread of Nuclear Weapons*, Congressional Research Service Report 83-94 S (Washington, D.C.: Library of Congress, 6 May 1983).
3. See Henry David Sokolski, *Eisenhower's Original Atoms for Peace Program: The Arms Control Connection*, Occasional Paper 52 (Washington, D.C.: Wilson Center, International Security Studies Program, 6 July 1983).
4. See Ty Cobb, "Soviet Proliferation Policy," paper presented before the Working Group on Small Nuclear Forces, Center for Strategic and International Studies, Summer 1983.
5. See Richard N. Holwill, "Market Forces and Nuclear Power," in *Agenda '83* (Washington, D.C.: Heritage Foundation, 1983).
6. Compare the testimony of Ronald Lehman before the Subcommittee on Energy, Nuclear Proliferation and Governmental Process, Senate Committee on Governmental Affairs, 13 May 1982.

4

Foreign Policy Preaching and Domestic Practice

Richard K. Lester

To most Americans who reflect on the matter, the further spread of nuclear weapons around the world is a profoundly disturbing prospect. Of those concerned with the foreign policy of the United States, many view the task of preventing nuclear weapons proliferation as transcending the national interest—even seeing it as a moral imperative. Yet, nuclear nonproliferation differs fundamentally from the other moral leitmotifs of twentieth-century U.S. foreign policy: the promotion and preservation of human rights, religious freedom, civil liberties, and so forth. The source of domestic political support for these latter goals, and of political opposition when the national interest is deemed to take precedence over them, is the deeply held view that rights enjoyed at home should be extended to others. Similarly, the confidence with which the United States lays international claim to moral authority in these matters derives from the example it sets at home.

Not so with the problem of nuclear proliferation. Though individual policymakers may be driven to act by an abhorrence of nuclear weapons and the possibility that they will be used, the United States as a nation can stake no claim to moral leadership in the struggle to prevent their spread. It pursues the goal of nonproliferation in parallel with its pursuit of a more effective national nuclear armament. Its government deplores the spread of nuclear weapons overseas while simultaneously stressing the military and political value of specific weapon systems for its own purposes. Its authority and influence in mitigating the risks of proliferation thus derive entirely from its standing as a global economic and military superpower. Its instruments are the tools of power, untempered by moral suasion: denial of technology; offers of economic cooperation, with political conditions attached; guarantees of security, often backed by its own nuclear forces. Inevitably, therefore, U.S. nonproliferation efforts are seen overseas to bear the stamp of *Realpolitik*, as being intended first and foremost to serve American national interests, whatever the individual motivations of those responsible for them.

Given the fundamental disjunction between its nuclear defense and nuclear nonproliferation postures, is there a rational case for the United States to seek consistency, however defined, between its domestic and nuclear power program and those elements of its nonproliferation policy which are intended to maximize the barriers between civilian and military nuclear activities overseas? In principle, there are two closely related kinds of proliferation-related considerations that might bear on the direction of domestic U.S. nuclear energy policy. First, the domestic nuclear power program preferably would not set technological precedents that, if followed by other countries, would bring them unacceptably close to the acquisition of nuclear weapons but, rather, would set an example that is technologically prudent (i.e., falling below some risk threshold) from a nonproliferation perspective. Second, the configuration of the domestic nuclear power program preferably would not be so different from that sought by the United States for foreign nuclear power programs as to handicap its international nonproliferation efforts. In practice, however, the usefulness of the first criterion would seem to depend on how strongly U.S. domestic nuclear energy policy decisions influence policymakers elsewhere, while the second will be useful only to the extent that consistency between U.S. domestic nuclear power policies and international nonproliferation goals is important to those whom the United States is trying to influence.

For most of America's first two decades of civilian nuclear energy development, such questions scarcely arose. Internationally, the United States was playing the leading role in developing a regime for nuclear energy development in which the principal barriers against the misuse of civilian technology were two: political undertakings by sovereign governments to desist from such activities and technical safeguards administered by the International Atomic Energy Agency (IAEA) to verify compliance. Further restrictions on civil nuclear activities were mostly not attempted and, indeed, were arguably precluded—at least as far as subscribers to the Nonproliferation Treaty (NPT) were concerned—by the terms of the treaty, which guarantees to its signatories that the peaceful exploitation of nuclear energy will not only remain unhindered, but also that it will actually be facilitated by the cooperation of the advanced nuclear nations.

At home, proliferation considerations played only a marginal role in the evolution of the U.S. nuclear power program. To be sure, the U.S. offer to apply international safeguards to a limited number of its commercial nuclear facilities—an offer originally extended by the Johnson administration but only recently implemented—was designed to strengthen the international nonproliferation regime. The primary intent here was not to verify that no civilian materials were being diverted to military ends but, rather, to allay international concern that the absence of any safeguards requirement would give the United States a commercial advantage over the non-nuclear-weapon states in the development of its nuclear energy industry. Proliferation considerations were also partly responsible for the practice of not using commercial nuclear energy facilities in the United States for military purposes. (A recent suggestion by the Reagan administration to use plutonium in spent power-reactor fuel for nuclear weapons production would, if implemented, constitute an important departure from that practice; and it is also worth noting that in two prominent cases facilities built originally for military purposes have been used for commercial applications.) But aside from these instances the question of shaping the domestic nuclear energy program of the United States so as to be consistent with the international regime largely did not arise.

In the mid-1970s, this situation changed. Concerns had begun to grow that the course of nuclear energy development on which most of the world had embarked, the United States included, would undermine the effectiveness of existing barriers to proliferation. That course would lead to the reprocessing of spent fuel from the first generation of reactors (mostly light-water reactors) and the recycling of the recovered uranium and plutonium to light-water reactors and, subsequently, in the case of the plutonium, to fast-breeder reactors. Exploitation of the plutonium in this way would vastly increase the energy value of natural uranium resources, thereby effectively eliminating fuel-resource constraints that would otherwise limit the economic lifetime of the nuclear energy option to a few decades. But with many reprocessing plants and large quantities of weapons-usable plutonium in commercial circulation throughout the world, it was feared, the international safeguards system would be incapable of detecting the diversion of the small amounts of plutonium needed to produce nuclear weapons. Moreover, the time needed to manufacture a weapon once the plutonium had been acquired would probably be too short for international preventive action to be effective, even if the diversion were immediately detected. Similar concerns applied to highly enriched uranium—another weapons-usable material—and to the spread of enrichment plants capable of producing it.

Responding to these concerns shortly before the 1976 election, President Ford, declaring that nonproliferation should take precedence over economic interests, recommended that spent-fuel reprocessing should no longer be regarded as inevitable and that it should be deferred throughout the world until more effective nonproliferation measures had been developed to deal with it. In line with this strategy, domestic commercial reprocessing—which until then had been expected to begin on a large scale before the end of the decade at a plant then nearing completion at Barnwell, South Carolina—was to be delayed. President Carter, extending this approach, announced in 1977 that domestic commercial reprocessing and plutonium recycling would be deferred "indefinitely," that the expected date of breeder commercialization would be delayed, and that the United States would launch a technological effort to develop new reactor and fuel-cycle systems offering less access to weapons-usable material. It was also made clear that the United States, through a combination of positive incentives and controls applied to its exports, would attempt to persuade other nations to adopt similar policies. The full extent of these measures became clear only in 1978, with the passage by Congress of the Nuclear Nonproliferation Act (NNPA), which unilaterally imposed even stricter conditions on U.S. exports than those originally sought by the administration.

Reactions Abroad

For the first time, the basic course of America's domestic nuclear energy program had been linked to the goal of preventing nuclear weapons proliferation. The rationale, of course, was that Washington's efforts to persuade others to defer reprocessing would be undermined unless U.S. industry followed suit and, further, that the new domestic fuel-cycle strategy would demonstrate to other nations the validity of the administration's argument that reprocessing was economically unnecessary and would remain so for many years to come.

Along with the rest of the Carter administration's nonproliferation policy, the domestic policy readjustment was strongly criticized overseas. Other governments argued vigorously that the U.S. "demonstration" of the new fuel-cycle economics was of little relevance to them; the bountiful endowment of fossil fuel and uranium resources bestowed upon the United States was contrasted with their own heavy dependence on energy imports and concerns over fuel-supply security. The demonstration effect was also weakened somewhat by the vocal demurrals of the U.S. nuclear industry, which hastened to explain to its counterparts overseas what it saw as the errors in the administration's position and the threat they posed to the industry as a whole.

The argument that the civilian nuclear fuel-cycle question could be approached only in a nondiscriminatory way, and that this in turn required the United States to forgo domestic reprocessing, was also strongly criticized overseas. The advanced industrialized nations of Western Europe and Japan implicitly (and sometimes explicitly) took issue with the alleged need for a nondiscriminatory approach. They argued variously that their own nonproliferation credentials, prior commitments to reprocessing, technological advancement, size, or (in the case of France and Britain) their nuclear weapons status should make them exempt from restrictions that, after all, were intended for other, less-reliable states. Consequently, they were unimpressed by

Washington's own renunciation of reprocessing. It was also pointed out that the U.S. commitment to a nondiscriminatory strategy was itself less than complete: centrifuge enrichment technology, considered by many to present at least as serious a proliferation risk as reprocessing technology and, like the latter, subject to a strict U.S. export embargo, had nonetheless been selected for the large commercial uranium-enrichment plant to be built by the government in the 1980s.

The principle of nondiscrimination in peaceful nuclear uses carried more weight with developing countries, owing to their greater reliance on technology transfer to gain access to the full benefits of nuclear power. The problem, from the perspective of these nations, was that the dividing line between acceptable and unacceptable nuclear applications had been redefined unilaterally. In this view, the U.S. renunciation of reprocessing was an act of voluntary self-denial and was in no way comparable to their own involuntary compliance with an externally imposed edict. Moreover, the attempt by the United States to gain broad adherence to its new fuel-cycle strategy was widely held to be inconsistent with the NPT.

That the domestic decision to forgo reprocessing was a necessary element of the new U.S. nonproliferation policy cannot seriously be disputed; without it, the international presentation of the policy would have been effectively impossible. But the response that this decision received would, on the face of it, seem to indicate that any additional contributions, in particular the hoped-for "demonstration effect," were at best marginal.

The reality may have been different, however. In the six years since the new U.S. policy was announced, there has been a growing international recognition both of the proliferation risks and the questionable economics of spent-fuel reprocessing and plutonium recycling. To be sure, the American attempt to secure a worldwide consensus in favor of a reprocessing deferral failed; plans to build large commercial reprocessing plants have proceeded in France and Britain, and reprocessing has continued on a smaller scale in Japan, Germany, and India. But overall the trend has been to move more slowly, and every country with a breeder-reactor development program of any size has announced significant delays in its development schedule within the past few years. Possibly this would have occurred anyway, irrespective of the U.S. intervention. In the years since the mid-1970s, economic conditions have become decidedly less favorable to the prompt recovery and recycle of plutonium; nuclear power plant construction programs have been scaled back drastically; and uranium demand and prices have fallen sharply. At the same time, the cost of reprocessing and recovery of the plutonium has escalated rapidly. Moreover, in at least one country—the Federal Republic of Germany—domestic environmental opposition was instrumental in the deferral of plans to build a large commercial reprocessing plant.

The impact of the U.S. actions is thus hard to gauge. Nevertheless, nuclear planners worldwide have not always been quick to respond to economic trends, and it is probable that the sharp change of course by the United States—at a time when it was still unquestionably the world's leading civil nuclear power—concentrated minds on the existence of alternatives to early reprocessing in a way that economic signals alone would not have done.

Ironically, the Reagan administration's early decisions to end its predecessor's moratorium on commercial reprocessing and to promote the development of a private reprocessing industry in the United States may actually have reinforced the international impact of the moratorium. For the subsequent unwillingness of the private sector to enter the field on a commercial basis has highlighted the economic unattractiveness of reprocessing at the present time.

There are several other links between domestic nuclear energy development in the United States and nuclear policies in other countries, not all of which are the planned results of specific policies. The most striking and significant trend within the U.S. nuclear power industry over the past several years has been the cessation of orders for new nuclear power plants and the deferral and cancellation of many previous orders. Though the impact is again difficult to gauge accurately (since many of the contributing problems are independently present in other countries), the difficulties experienced in the United States have almost certainly had negative repercussions for nuclear power programs abroad, just as in previous decades the rapid growth of the American program provided a stimulus to nuclear development efforts elsewhere. Today, of course, electric-power planners in countries considering nuclear commitments are subject to a broader range of international influences, at least some of which are more reassuring than those emanating from the United States. Still, the continuing reports from the United States of cost overruns, management problems, plant cancellations, poor operating statistics, financial weaknesses, and regulatory problems must be a source of concern, if not discouragement.

Moreover, though government and industry officials overseas are careful to draw distinctions between their own economic-political circumstances and technological competences and those of the United States, public opinion in these countries may be less discriminatory, especially given the American origin of the light-water reactor technology in almost universal use today. In Western Europe and Japan, where public opinion bears heavily on nuclear decisionmaking, officials bemoan the boost to their domestic critics' credibility provided by events in the United States.

Another important linkage has to do with the problem of technological innovation on the very large scale required to commercialize the next generation of nuclear systems. In previous years, other nations benefited from the ability and predisposition of the United States, with its vast economy and electric-power markets, to assume much of the risks and cost of civil nuclear development. But the economic difficulties confronting nuclear power and the erosion in domestic support for the nuclear option are undermining the traditional commitment of the United States to maintain its technological leadership in the field, as Congress's decision to terminate funding for the Clinch River breeder reactor showed. At the same time, research and development costs continue to mount. Although international cost- and risk-sharing arrangements can to some extent offset these trends—and indeed are playing an increasingly important role in nuclear R&D worldwide—a diminished American willingness to share the burdens of development may significantly impair parallel efforts overseas.

The Political Prognosis

The effect of all this on the risks of further proliferation is debatable. A slower pace of nuclear power growth worldwide allows more time to develop effective international arrangements for the control of new fuel-cycle technologies. But the gains may only be marginal if governments merely convert their earlier plans for commercialization into extended (and more easily justified) development and demonstration programs. Furthermore, additional obstacles to nuclear power growth in the advanced industrialized countries add to the pressures on their nuclear supply industries to find new export markets, increasing the risk that existing supplier restraints on the export of sensitive technology and material will be eroded.

But although the reverberations of the present nuclear energy crisis in the United States are widely felt, the interdependence of national nuclear energy programs is not unlimited. In the long run the international nuclear power industry would certainly survive even the permanent demise of the American nuclear energy option. In fact, such a scenario is becoming less and less implausible, and its implications for the international nonproliferation regime deserve careful consideration.

Even in the worst case for the American nuclear industry domestically, the decline of industrial capacity would be quite gradual. For many years to come—whatever the outcome of the domestic policy debate—most of the major nuclear engineering and manufacturing firms will remain active, both in domestic and overseas markets, as purveyors of maintenance, repair, retrofitting, and other services to operating commercial plants and those now under construction. Moreover, the two primary nuclear reactor vendors, Westinghouse and General Electric, will seek to preserve at least a residual capability to meet future international orders for as long as possible—although for both companies the trend will increasingly be to form partnerships with past and present licensees (and potential rivals) in which design and manufacturing work will be shared internationally. In the long run, though, it seems improbable that the U.S. nuclear industry would be able to retain a significant share of the international market in the absence of an active domestic base of operations.

The industrial scenario sketched here—merely a continuation of international trends that have been evident for several years—has potentially profound implications for the future international nonproliferation regime. This political-legal structure, whose two central pillars are the international safeguards system and the NPT, is based on a principle first advanced by the United States in the 1950s under the Atoms for Peace program: assistance and cooperation in civil nuclear development will be provided in return for externally verified assurances by recipient governments that civilian nuclear materials or technology will not be diverted to military ends. The present regime is very much the product of this American conception, and its creation would have been inconceivable without the promotional efforts of the United States. Other contributions were also important, of course; the political support of the Soviet Union, especially, was indispensable. But the crucial factor was the historical convergence within the United States of the global security interests of a nuclear superpower, powerful political interests promoting the commercial exploitation of nuclear energy, and the technological and industrial capacity to make the United States the world leader in civil nuclear development and cooperation. This, in effect, allowed much of the debate over the appropriate balance between security concerns and economic benefits to be internalized within the United States. The same issues had to be rehearsed in international forums, of course, and those negotiations forced the United States to revise some of its thinking and accept additional obligations. But the strength and enthusiasm of the American nuclear industry—the solid evidence, as it were, of the U.S. ability to deliver on its political promises of peaceful nuclear cooperation—did much to facilitate international acceptance of the general outlines of the American position.

Today, however, we confront the prospect of a growing international separation of global security interests from the commercial interests of civil nuclear industries. With the American nuclear industry in decline, industrial leadership is passing to the middle powers—the European nations and Japan (whose previous inactivity in nuclear export markets does not reflect either its current industrial capabilities or its future intentions). These nations have global economic interests but, usually, more narrowly defined security concerns, and their governments may be less able or less willing to meet the international political responsibilities that come with nuclear industrial leadership. Within the United States, moreover, it seems probable that the political influence of the nuclear industry and its supporters will ebb as the commercial outlook worsens. That internal political shift will be reflected in the international posture adopted by the United States on questions of nuclear commerce.

Thus, although the Reagan administration's support for a liberal nuclear-trading regime is stronger than that of its predecessor, the secular political trend may well be in the opposite direction.

None of this bodes well for efforts to achieve an international consensus on strengthening the global nonproliferation regime or for relations between the United States and its industrial allies. There is, however, one practical domestic policy measure available to the United States, at least in principle, whose impact on the risks of proliferation would be unambiguously positive, whose adoption need not be tied to the future viability of the domestic nuclear energy option, and whose effect would be to strengthen rather than strain America's relations with its allies and nuclear trading partners.

As of today, possibly the single most constructive unilateral contribution the United States could make toward the separation of peaceful and military uses of nuclear energy would be to develop the capability to accept foreign spent fuel for storage and final disposal. In several countries, shortages of storage capacity for spent fuel are beginning to pose problems, and in some cases are generating additional pressures to initiate reprocessing. Suitable sites for repositories for high-level waste are likely to be in critically short supply. A U.S. commitment to accept spent fuel from overseas would help to reduce further incentives to reprocess, and, in addition, would provide the United States with new opportunities to influence the direction of foreign nuclear power programs at a time when the traditional sources of leverage—nuclear fuel and equipment exports—are slipping away as the U.S. share of the international market in these areas declines.

The domestic political obstacles that would have to be overcome before such a commitment could be made would, of course, be formidable. Previous efforts to provide domestic storage capacity for foreign commercial spent fuel have failed to win much support in Congress, primarily because of concern over the perceived environmental costs of such a policy and the political costs to those who supported it. The Nuclear Nonproliferation Act of 1978 authorizes the president to accept limited quantities of foreign spent fuel without congressional approval, but only in emergency situations and when it is determined to be in the national interest to do so. A later attempt to incorporate into the Nuclear Waste Policy Act of 1982 a provision that would have allowed the Department of Energy to store a small quantity of foreign spent fuel was defeated.

In the longer run, however, as the domestic management program for high-level waste moves ahead, the idea of taking in foreign spent fuel could become more acceptable politically or, at least, less unacceptable. If the amounts involved are modest compared with domestic waste inventories, this would be even more likely. (Even if all the spent fuel generated by all nations outside Comecon and the Organization for Economic Cooperation and Development was taken in, the increment would amount to only a modest fraction of the spent fuel produced domestically.) There is also the prospect of substantial revenues flowing to the United States from such a scheme. In the final analysis, however, the feasibility of the scheme will depend on whether the perceived environmental costs associated with it would be offset by its perceived contribution to the goal of nonproliferation. In turn, the latter will largely depend on whether those countries from which the removal of spent fuel would be most desirable on security grounds would in fact be willing to participate. Even the participation of other nations would be helpful, however, to the extent that it strengthened international norms against premature, uneconomic reprocessing.

Ideally, an international program for storing spent power-reactor fuel would involve several host nations. In the meantime, however, a unilateral initiative by the United States deserves serious consideration. Indeed, if the recent decline in the health of the U.S. nuclear industry persists indefinitely, storing the spent fuel of other nations may ultimately offer the only avenue for continued U.S. participation in the international regime for controlling the peaceful uses of atomic energy.

5

Congressional Interest and Input

Warren H. Donnelly

Ever since 1945, when the United States used the atom bomb to end the war in the Pacific, the executive branch and Congress have had a continuing interest in ways and means to limit the further spread, or proliferation, of nuclear weapons. At times, Congress has been the prime mover, as in enactment of the Atomic Energy Acts of 1946 and 1954, and of the Nuclear Nonproliferation Act of 1978 (NNPA). At other times, the executive branch has taken the lead, as with negotiation of the Treaty on the Nonproliferation of Nuclear Weapons (NPT) in the late 1960s and the Nuclear Suppliers Group guidelines in the mid-1970s.

Changing Congressional Interest

While congressional interest in nonproliferation policy has been evident since the 1940s, the 1970s were propitious for efforts by Congress to exert influence in this sphere. Its suspicions of the executive branch had been stirred by controversies over Vietnam and Watergate at the beginning of the decade; by the end of the decade, Congress was able to curtail the unrestrained freedom of the executive branch to carry out the vaguely stated policies of the Atomic Energy Act of 1954.

Congressional nonproliferation interests were further amplified during the decade by pressures from the expanding environmental movement, which included a strong antinuclear plank. This was to bring down the powerful Atomic Energy Commission (AEC). The Energy Reorganization Act of 1974 abolished the AEC and divided its responsibilities between the new Energy

The views expressed here are those of the authors and not necessarily those of the Congressional Research Service.

Research and Development Administration (ERDA), later to become the Department of Energy (DOE), and the new Nuclear Regulatory Commission (NRC).

Congressional efforts to influence executive branch thinking about non-proliferation policy in the 1970s began with hearings a few weeks after President Nixon's visit to the Middle East during the oil crisis of 1974. Nixon's announcement that the United States was ready to enter into agreements for nuclear cooperation with Egypt and Israel spurred two subcommittees of the House Committee on Foreign Affairs to hold hearings on U.S. foreign policy and the export of nuclear technology to the Middle East. Subsequently, the subcommittee chairmen, Donald M. Fraser and Lee H. Hamilton, issued a joint statement expressing concern over future risks of proliferation, arguing that the United States must immediately prepare for an era of inevitable proliferation of nuclear technology. In their view, existing safeguards machinery and associated organizational support needed to be reconsidered and strengthened. They proposed a four-point program to have the United States initiate negotiations with all other nuclear exporters to establish a universal system of safeguards; use U.S. leverage to urge as many states as possible to sign and ratify the NPT; work for the adoption of a comprehensive test ban treaty; and seek to strengthen the International Atomic Energy Agency (IAEA). Other House interest appeared in hearings called by Representative Jonathan Bingham, chairman of the Committee on International Affairs, and by Representative Morris Udall, chairman of the Committee on Interior and Insular Affairs.

In the Senate, the center of early interest was in a subcommittee of the Committee on Banking, Housing and Urban Affairs. On 12 July 1974, it held a hearing on export policy, control, and credits, with particular attention to exports of nuclear technology and nuclear materials. Senator Adlai Stevenson's statement in opening the hearings gives a good sense of the contemporary views of congressional critics of U.S. policy. He said that nuclear proliferation was one of the greatest threats to world peace and security. If nuclear weapons were possessed by many nations, Stevenson argued, the "balance of terror" could be destabilized and all hopes for nuclear arms reductions destroyed. Moreover, the uncontrolled spread of nuclear technology and materials could disrupt relations among nations and make nuclear blackmail by terrorist organizations a real possibility. He blasted U.S. nuclear export policy, saying that the United States had neither a coherent nuclear export policy nor coherent procedures for controlling nuclear exports. Because the United States was seemingly promoting indiscriminate sales of nuclear facilities abroad, it faced the growing dangers of international blackmail by nuclear terrorists, nuclear holocaust, and the poisoning of the atmosphere.

Senator Stuart Symington was also a strong critic of weaknesses in U.S.

nonproliferation policy, and later put through legislation to cut off certain U.S. economic and military assistance to countries that imported or exported items for reprocessing or enrichment plants under certain circumstances. It was in the Committee on Government Operations under Senator Abraham Ribicoff, however, that continuing Senate interest in nonproliferation took root and flowered. Ribicoff soon established a new subcommittee, chaired by former astronaut Senator John Glenn, with nonproliferation as a primary responsibility. This provided Senators Glenn and Charles Percy with a base of operations.

A steady stream of bills and further hearings kept congressional interest in nonproliferation high and maintained pressure on the Nixon and Ford administrations. Early in his term, President Carter preempted the nonproliferation issue by his strong statement of policy on 7 April 1977 and subsequent legislative proposals. Working behind the scenes, his administration was able partially to influence the drafting of the legislation that became the Nuclear Nonproliferation Act of 1978. But Congress had its way with some points and insisted on provisions not contained in the Carter draft.

With the NNPA enacted, there was a natural falling off both of congressional concern about proliferation and specific congressional efforts to influence nonproliferation policy. Nonetheless, congressional fears of further nuclear weapons spread were not laid to rest. Even before the mid-point of the Carter administration, some voices had begun to criticize its implementation of the new act. The Reagan administration in its turn is now facing such congressional criticism and a more complicated congressional situation because, unlike the Carter administration, its party does not have a majority in both houses.

Frequent Themes in Congress

In the continuing congressional efforts to influence U.S. nonproliferation policy, we witness several themes with notable durability. Most significant are those spotlighting executive-legislative differences. The separation of nonproliferation from foreign policy, which touches on executive flexibility, is one such theme. During hearings that led to the NNPA, it became the view of some members that U.S. nonproliferation policy had to take precedence over and be kept separate from foreign policy, rather than the reverse. It was important that U.S. nonproliferation policy and its application not become a "bargaining chip," with the prospect that it might be sacrificed to allow executive branch flexibility in negotiations with other countries. This view was not shared by the executive branch, as was made abundantly clear by Secretary of State Henry Kissinger in a 1976 hearing.

A second theme, which explains some of the tension between Congress and various administrations over U.S. nonproliferation policy, involves the desire of some members to expand the definition of "proliferation." The NPT confined proliferation to the actual testing and acquisition of nuclear weapons. Nothing in it limits non-nuclear-weapon states in their choice of nuclear fuels for civilian nuclear power, or construction of facilities to produce them. However, since the mid-1970s there has been a renewed uneasiness among some members of Congress about the potential spread of nuclear materials that are directly useful in making nuclear weapons, notably plutonium and highly enriched uranium, and the facilities to produce them. This view is evident in the NNPA.

It follows logically from an expanded definition of "proliferation" that commercial production and use of plutonium as a nuclear fuel should be avoided and discouraged. This third theme reflects a view that would treat all grades of plutonium as equally useful in making nuclear explosives or weapons. Echoes of this argument are heard in the refusal of Congress to fund construction of the Clinch River breeder reactor demonstration; opposition to completion and operation of the privately owned Barnwell nuclear-fuel reprocessing plant; use of plutonium in conventional nuclear power reactors (recycle); foreign reprocessing of U.S.-controlled spent fuel; and U.S. technical assistance for construction of reprocessing plants abroad, notably in Japan.

From this viewpoint, the commercial production and use of plutonium as a fuel will be unnecessary for many years because the projections for future growth of world nuclear power generation and consequent demand for nuclear fuel have dropped dramatically; uranium production and enrichment capacities are ample to fuel all of the nuclear power plants that are likely to be built for many years to come; the efficiency of conventional nuclear power plants in their use of uranium can be substantially increased, thereby reducing the amount of fuel needed; and concern about the adequacy of international inspection to verify that there has been no diversion of plutonium, and of the international sanctions to be applied should diversion be discovered.

Another frequently heard theme is denial. The idea is simply to prevent, or to make difficult, non-nuclear-weapon states' construction of facilities to produce plutonium and highly enriched uranium. It is argued that the fewer the number of sensitive facilities in non-nuclear-weapon states for reprocessing, enrichment, and heavy water production, the less the chance that these might be diverted from peaceful purposes, particularly in states whose nuclear ambitions and activities are viewed with suspicion. Some in Congress would have the executive branch seek stronger commitments by nuclear suppliers not to supply such sensitive facilities. Others would ban all nuclear commerce in the hope of preventing a further spread of the industrial base useful for fabrication of nuclear weapons. Note that proponents of denial tend to doubt the adequacy of the NPT's no-weapons pledges and to discount the commitment of the United States under the NPT to assist other NPT states with nuclear energy.

An occasional theme in congressional thinking is the inadequacy of present sanctions to deter countries from breaking their nonproliferation commitments. The international statute that established the IAEA would punish a violation of an IAEA safeguards agreement by cutting off nuclear cooperation to the state involved and reporting it to the members of the agency as well as to the United Nations Security Council and General Assembly. These responses are often viewed as ineffectual. Indeed, this was one argument advanced by Israel to justify its bombing of Iraq's large research reactor in 1981. U.S. nonproliferation policy goes further by mandating the cutoff of U.S. nuclear cooperation to non-nuclear-weapon states that violate agreements or test nuclear explosives and, in some circumstances, the cutoff of certain U.S. economic and military assistance to states that import or supply the wherewithal to build enrichment or reprocessing plants, or test or receive a nuclear explosive.

Even less frequently heard is the theme that the United States, with or without the cooperation of other suppliers, should offer incentives to obtain acceptance of U.S. policies from other states. The linkage between reliability in supply and in adherence to nonproliferation commitments was underscored by the International Nuclear Fuel Cycle Evaluation in 1980, which noted as a general principle that assurances of supply and of nonproliferation are complementary. Offsetting this, however, is the proposition, strong in Congress, that the United States should vigorously use whatever influence (leverage) it has through veiled or overt threats to cut off U.S. nuclear cooperation to states that do not agree to U.S. policies.

A new theme in Congress is the suspicion that plutonium recovered from spent fuel of civil nuclear power plants might be diverted to production of weapons. This appeared in 1981 soon after the secretary of energy hinted that DOE was considering recovery of plutonium from commercial spent fuel as one way to expand the supply of plutonium required for increased nuclear weapons production. This led to various legislative initiatives, culminating in legislation to prevent the NRC from licensing the transfer of spent fuel from its licensees to the Department of Energy for military purposes. However, this ban did not extend to spent fuel from the DOE's fast flux test reactor or from the big dual-purpose reactor at Richland, Washington, which generates electricity and produces plutonium. So this theme is likely to remain quite lively. A similar concern questions the wisdom of permitting use of U.S.-controlled plutonium in the French breeder development program without an explicit French commitment not to use any of this plutonium for weapons.

From time to time the suggestion is made in the executive branch, or in academic circles, that one way to avoid the further spread of nuclear weapons is to reduce the reasons that a government might want them. This approach has to rely more upon a combination of tendencies in international relations, and active diplomacy and offers of security assurances than upon denial of access to sensitive nuclear technologies. Not surprisingly, congressional activists have shown little interest in this approach. Many reasons may be involved, but we need only note that this political route depends upon executive branch exercise of its foreign relations powers, an area not readily accessible to the reach of Congress.

The 97th Congress and the Reagan Administration

During the first two years of the Reagan administration, there were many legislative and other congressional actions to tighten U.S. policy for nuclear cooperation and trade, and to strengthen general nonproliferation measures. These activities mark the struggle in some quarters of Congress to continue to shape the further evolution of U.S. nonproliferation policy. Among them, the most tangible is complete legislation, which represents Congress as a whole. Then come proposals for new legislation and congressional advice, and the response of Congress to external events, such as Israel's bombing of Iraq's research reactor in 1981 or the IAEA General Conference's denial of the credentials of Israel's delegation in 1982.

Several resolutions expressing the sense of Congress were passed by the 97th Congress. Perhaps the most notable were those that sought to get President Reagan to take up nonproliferation at the economic summit conferences at Ottawa in 1981 and at Versailles in 1982.[1] Going beyond the advisory resolutions were several public laws. The latter included measures to permit resumption of U.S. economic and military aid to Pakistan; to condition U.S. funding to the IAEA upon the continued participation of Israel in agency activities; and to prevent the Department of Energy from using commercial spent nuclear fuel for military purposes.

The amendment of the Symington-Glenn amendments to the Foreign Assistance Act, which had caused the Carter administration to cut off certain U.S. economic and military aid to Pakistan because that country had persisted in trying to import parts for an enrichment plant, was especially notable. After the Soviet invasion of Afghanistan, the Carter and later the Reagan administrations sought to resume U.S. aid, even though Pakistan declined to stop its enrichment efforts and unequivocally to agree not to make nuclear weapons. The Reagan administration finally put through the International Security and Development Cooperation Act of 1981, which temporarily waived the aid cutoff, but added a new cutoff for any country that transfers a nuclear explosive device to a non-nuclear-weapon state, or to any non-nuclear-weapon state that receives or detonates such a device. An earlier version would also have included possession of nuclear weapons as cause for a cutoff, but this provision was deleted because some members thought it might apply to Israel.

The reaction of Congress to external events is exemplified by its response to the denial of Israel's credentials by the IAEA's General Conference in September 1982, an action deemed illegal by the United States. As a result, the U.S. delegation walked out of the conference, and the executive branch began an assessment of its relations with the agency. In December 1982, while the assessment was still in progress, Senators Robert Kasten and James McClure attached an amendment to the continuing appropriation for FY 1983 to prohibit the use of funds appropriated for payment to the IAEA unless its Board of Governors certified to the United States that Israel is allowed to participate fully as a member nation in the activities of the agency. Finding ways to comply with this amendment delayed U.S. resumption of its relations with the agency until the Board of Governors meeting of 22 February 1983.

Congressional concern in 1981 that plutonium in spent fuel from nuclear power plants might be recovered and used for military purposes culminated in an amendment to the authorization of the Nuclear Regulatory Commission for fiscal years 1981 and 1982. The amendment prevents the NRC from licensing the transfer of spent fuel or plutonium recovered from it to DOE for military purposes. The effect of this amendment is not only to cut off direct use of commercial plutonium for weapons but also to prevent its use from releasing higher-grade DOE plutonium from energy research and development to make nuclear weapons.

The efforts of the 97th Congress to shape further U.S. nonproliferation policy are also visible in resolutions and bills that were introduced but never passed. The 97th Congress received about forty such proposals during 1981-82; notable were those of Senators Arlen Specter and Gary Hart, and Representatives Jonathan Bingham, Richard Ottinger, and Howard Wolpe. Because of reports that the administration had adopted a more lenient policy for sale of nuclear materials and technology, Senator Specter proposed to restrict nuclear sales to "irresponsible nations" by requiring congressional review of any application for nuclear exports to any country that has not joined the NPT.[2] Senator Hart introduced several bills. In 1981, he proposed amendments to the NNPA to discourage and prevent the commercial use of plutonium for fuel; to prohibit U.S. nuclear exports to any country without a reprocessing capability until that country would agree not to obtain or to use such a capacity, or to seek access to separated plutonium; to prohibit any U.S. nuclear exports until the president reports to Congress in detail on U.S. nonproliferation policy, and certifies that "such policy will significantly reduce the risks of nuclear proliferation," and Congress approves the report; and to prohibit approval for the reprocessing abroad of spent fuel controlled by the United States.[3] In April 1982, he proposed a joint resolution to call for negotiation of a halt to all plutonium production for any purpose and the export of its means of production, and for international rejection of the commercial use of separated plutonium as a nuclear fuel.[4]

More substantial interest appeared in major amendments to the NNPA proposed in 1982 by Senators Hart and William Proxmire and by Representatives Ottinger and Bingham. Common to all of these bills was tighter control, even prohibition in some instances, of U.S. export of sensitive nuclear materials and of related technologies, equipment, and supplies. Two items are especially noteworthy: a proposal to cut off U.S. nuclear cooperation to states that will not agree to U.S. nonproliferation policies; and the continued emphasis upon full-scope safeguards as a condition for all U.S. nuclear export, and for those of other suppliers.

The Struggle Continues

The story of the struggle by some quarters of Congress to continue to shape the further evolution of U.S. nonproliferation policy did not end with the 97th Congress; it continued into the 98th Congress. Echoes of it were heard during the presidential campaign of 1984. The struggle continues over peripheral matters, for there is agreement between Congress and the Reagan administration that further spread of nuclear weapons clearly is not in the best interests of the United States or of world peace. The administration is also agreed that the spread of sensitive nuclear activities, such as reprocessing and enrichment, is clearly undesirable in non-nuclear-weapon states that have no economic reason for them, that are not advanced in nuclear power technology and generation, and that are proliferation risks. To the extent that the major differences between the Congress and the executive cannot be attributed to institutional interests and attitudes, they concern the question of whether all U.S. nuclear partners should be treated identically without regard to circumstances, or whether U.S. nuclear cooperation should be tailored to differing situations.

Soon after the 98th Congress convened in 1983, the principal bills to amend the NNPA of the preceding Congress were reintroduced, along with the Nuclear Explosives Control Act of 1983, but none of these bills saw further action. Instead, the legislative drive has been limited to attempts to plug what are seen as loopholes in the NNPA, which permit exports of certain minor items and technical cooperation to states that will not join the NPT nor agree to full-scope safeguards. This legislative activity appears in amendments to the Export Administration Act Amendments of 1984, which remained mired in conference.

Some congressional members and offices continue to express concern that the Reagan administration favors the commercialization of plutonium, and that the United States might damage its nonproliferation influence by blurring the line between civil and military plutonium in this country or acquiescing to such a blurring in other nuclear-weapon states. Indications of this concern appeared in efforts by Congressman Ottinger in the House Committee on Energy and Commerce to prohibit the Department of Energy from transferring plutonium used in its civil research and development programs to military uses, and his attempts to obtain from the secretary of energy an unequivocal statement that DOE would not use any plutonium of British origin for military purposes. This concern was also reflected in questions of other members about whether U.S.-controlled plutonium owned by various states and now held in France would be transferred to the French breeder program, particularly to Super-Phénix. These members point to an apparent unwillingness by France to agree that none of the plutonium produced by this breeder will be used to make French nuclear weapons. Other matters that continue to attract congressional interest include nuclear assistance to India, either directly by the United States or indirectly by other countries, notably France; brokering by U.S. companies to arrange for supplies of enriched uranium to states not eligible for U.S. nuclear exports; the inclusion of provisions for long-term, or programmatic, approval of reprocessing in new or amended agreements for U.S. nuclear cooperation; and the provisions of the U.S.-Chinese nuclear cooperation agreement, and the extent to which they satisfy U.S. statutory requirements.

Dealing with these matters requires some considerable knowledge of proliferation risks and U.S. policy for nuclear cooperation and trade. Because such knowledge is not widely spread among the public, it is difficult for members to make proliferation issues public. However, one comparatively simple nonproliferation proposal likely to be featured in the 99th Congress would halt the production of separated plutonium. Senator Hart introduced such a resolution in 1982 and again in 1983.[5] At the time of writing, the Democratic party platform for the campaign had not been concluded but was expected to include Senator Hart's proposal. Also, in his keynote speech at the Democratic National Convention, Governor Mario Cuomo said that "we proclaim as loudly as we can the utter insanity of nuclear proliferation and the need for nuclear freeze, if only to affirm the simple truth that peace is better than war because life is better than death."[6]

So there is good reason to expect that the interest of Congress in ways and means of avoiding further proliferation will continue, as will its struggle to influence future U.S. nonproliferation policy.

Notes

1. See House Resolution 177 and Senate Resolution 179 (17 July 1981); and House Concurrent Resolution 340 (20 May 1982) and Senate Concurrent Resolution 96 (27 May 1982).
2. S. 2563, Nuclear Material Export Control Act of 1982 (24 May 1982).

3. S. 1488, Nuclear Non-Proliferation Act Amendments of 1981 (15 July 1981).
4. Senate Joint Resolution 192 (27 April 1982).
5. See Senate Joint Resolution 192 (27 April 1982); and Senate Joint Resolution 124 (27 June 1983).
6. *New York Times*, 17 July 1984.

6

Congressional Counterattack: Reagan and the Congress

John Maxwell Hamilton and Leonard S. Spector

In September 1982, before a small audience made up almost exclusively of executive branch officials, the House Subcommittee on International Economic Policy and Trade met to consider a series of amendments to the 1978 Nuclear Nonproliferation Act (NNPA). In the space of only a few minutes, the members voted unanimously for all the legislative changes, each of which the Reagan administration strongly opposed. The vote was a repudiation of President Reagan's nuclear nonproliferation policies. Indeed, several provisions of the bill were specifically designed to thwart the administration's professed goal of stepping up U.S. nuclear exports. Despite this, the subcommittee action received scant attention from the press and made virtually no impression on the public at large.

Surprising as this response may seem in the light of intense public concern over the Reagan administration's nuclear arms policies, it is part of a pattern. During the 97th Congress (1981-82) the executive branch determinedly sought to loosen commercial nuclear export controls without provoking a public outcry that it was soft on nuclear proliferation. With equal determination, and often as quietly, influential members of the House and Senate fought back for more restrictive nuclear policies.

Well-publicized battles between Congress and the executive branch rarely leave clear-cut winners and losers, and it is difficult to pick out the victors of behind-the-scenes conflicts. In one sense, the failure of Congress to pass NNPA amendments into law before the end of the session was a victory for the administration. Nevertheless, it is clear that although Reagan succeeded in loosening nuclear trade restraints in individual instances, Congress—using the oversight process and, when feasible, legislative mandate—largely checked Reagan's attacks on nuclear export policies put into place during the Carter years. And the pattern continued into the 98th Congress. In 1983 and 1984, both the House and the Senate vigorously pursued key amendments previously passed by the Subcommittee on International Economic Policy and Trade.

Legislation

The best measure of the success of Congress has been its preservation of the basic law governing U.S. nonproliferation activities, the NNPA. Shortly after Reagan's election, a transition team on nonproliferation policy, chaired by Richard T. Kennedy and James L. Malone, who would become the senior nonproliferation officials in the new administration, put together a report recommending a series of major changes in the U.S. nonproliferation program. Included was a two-page list of proposed modifications of the NNPA intended expressly to minimize "the need for Congressional review of Executive Branch actions." The revisions were not cosmetic but were aimed at provisions central to the act. In particular, the report proposed the repeal of the NNPA's prohibition on exporting nuclear fuel and reactors to nations that have not accepted International Atomic Energy Agency (IAEA) inspections on all their nuclear installations—i.e. "full-scope inspections"—and a relaxation of NNPA constraints on U.S. approvals for the reprocessing abroad of U.S.-origin spent reactor fuel to extract plutonium (which can be used for nuclear weapons as well as for fuel). To accomplish this, the Reagan team called for the immediate formulation of an aggressive legislative strategy and for preparation of a draft bill amending the NNPA at the "earliest date possible."[1]

Events were to unfold differently in the ensuing months. The administration's first major pronouncement on nonproliferation, Reagan's statement on nonproliferation and peaceful nuclear cooperation policy on 16 July 1981, announced no legislative initiatives but called instead for further "review" of existing laws to determine what changes, if any, should be proposed. In mid-November 1981—nearly a year after the transition team report—Malone testified on Capitol Hill that the review was still "far from the stage where the administration could say whether any such changes may be desirable," and that it did "not anticipate submitting any proposals in the near term."[2] And in May 1982, the administration abandoned the idea of revising U.S. nonproliferation laws. At a Senate hearing, Under Secretary of State Kennedy testified that "a consensus was reached [within the administration] to postpone consideration of changes to the law for the time being" and that the administration had "decided not to submit proposed legislation to change the NNPA."[3] Kennedy claimed that this decision had been taken to avoid the impression of instability in U.S. nonproliferation policymaking. That assertion, however, seemed calculated to put a bright gloss on the true reason for the administration's change of attitude: the dim prospects for winning approval of NNPA amendments on Capitol Hill.

Numerous factors contributed to this situation. One, clearly, was the president himself. While President Carter had devoted considerable personal attention to promoting tougher nonproliferation controls, Reagan, consumed by domestic concerns, appeared unwilling to offer more than perfunctory rhetoric on this issue. In addition, the administration confronted a formidable array of roadblocks: a steady stream of criticism by House and Senate opinion leaders; hearings probing the effect of administration nonproliferation decisions that would loosen constraints on plutonium use and nuclear transfers; controversy surrounding the ties to the nuclear industry of Malone, the administration's appointee to run U.S. nonproliferation policy on a day-to-day basis; and an unexpectedly positive General Accounting Office report on the NNPA's effectiveness.[4]

Four events involving Congress stand out as especially damaging to the administration's hopes for statutory changes: the 7 June 1981 Israeli raid that destroyed Iraq's research reactor near Baghdad; the premature disclosure of a State Department strategy document for implementing major changes in U.S. nonproliferation laws and policy; and two clear-cut legislative defeats, the first thwarting administration efforts to emasculate the provisions of the 1961 Foreign Assistance Act, which prohibited U.S. economic and military assistance to nations engaging in certain provocative nuclear activities, and the second, blocking an administration proposal to use plutonium from civilian nuclear power plants for United States nuclear weapons.

The Israeli raid made headlines around the world and triggered a widely reported series of congressional hearings publicizing weaknesses in the international nonproliferation regime. The hearings brought out two points with particular force: the importance of applying full-scope inspections by the IAEA (Iraq had facilities that, because of technicalities, had not yet come under this regime) and the inherent dangers of reprocessing (Israel believed that Iraq's Nonproliferation Treaty pledge not to build nuclear weapons would be insufficient protection once Iraq could use its small-scale reprocessing capability to separate weapons-usable plutonium). The lesson seemed to be that tougher, not weaker, nonproliferation controls were needed in the very areas the transition team report had targeted for weakening NNPA amendments. Rather than endorsing nascent administration export policies, both houses of Congress unanimously passed resolutions in July 1981 calling on the president to take up measures for tightening international nuclear controls with allied leaders at the upcoming Ottawa summit.[5] It is perhaps not surprising, then, that Reagan's nonproliferation policy statement three days earlier did not include proposals for modifying existing nonproliferation laws along the lines originally proposed by his advisers.

Despite these setbacks, the Reagan administration had not, apparently, given up hope of amending the NNPA. In the fall, an interagency working group on nonproliferation and peaceful nuclear cooperation policies, chaired by Malone, met to consider possible amendments. Among the proposals outlined in a confidential discussion paper dated 2 October 1981 was the "transfer of the export licensing functions from the Nuclear Regulatory Commission [NRC] to the Department of State [and] the elimination of the retroactive application of the nuclear export criteria established by the Nuclear Non-Proliferation Act of 1978."[6] The former would have relieved the independent NRC of its responsibility to approve executive branch export decisions, thus giving the State Department considerably greater freedom of action in implementing nonproliferation policy. The latter would have permitted nuclear exports to India, South Africa, Brazil, and Argentina—all countries not permitting the full-scope IAEA inspections required in the NNPA as a condition of United States nuclear supply.

The discussion paper specified "strong Congressional opposition" as the chief argument against such amendments, and noted that a "major effort by the Administration will be required to succeed." This turned out to be prophetic. When the document was disclosed by the press on 11 October 1981, it became a major embarrassment to the administration, forcing it back on the defensive once again. Legislators used the occasion to attack the Reagan nuclear policies—Senator John Glenn, for one, calling them "toothless." The administration, Glenn said, saw nuclear trade abroad as "just another business development like selling automobiles or washing machines."[7] State Department officials claimed the Malone memo was only a "discussion paper," not a statement of administration policy having united interagency support.[8] It may have been for just this reason that the congressional outcry over the Malone memo seemed to have a preemptive impact on the executive branch's long-stated plan to modify the NNPA, leading to Malone's November 1981 testimony, quoted above, that the "review" of nonproliferation laws ordered by the president in July was still far from complete.

Administration efforts to provide aid to Pakistan in the closing months of 1981 resulted in the clearest congressional opposition to a wholesale relaxation of U.S. nonproliferation restrictions. Aid for Pakistan had wide support. Secretary of State Alexander Haig and many in Congress considered it essential to U.S. strategic interests to shore up the Zia regime against the threat of Soviet troops in Afghanistan. Reagan's nonproliferation officials claimed that only through increased U.S. conventional arms support could Pakistan be persuaded that it did not need nuclear weapons to protect itself. In all, the administration hoped to provide Pakistan with some $3.2 billion in economic and military assistance (including forty F-16 fighters) during the course of six years.

Notwithstanding the concern about Soviet adventurism in the Persian Gulf region, Section 669 of the 1961 Foreign Assistance Act prohibited such aid to Pakistan. This provision, added to the act as the "Symington amendment" in 1976, stated that the United States could not give economic or military assistance to any nation that imported uranium enrichment technology unless that nation agreed to full-scope IAEA inspections. Pakistan, known to have imported such technology, had refused to permit the necessary safeguards. The amendment contained a proviso allowing the president to waive the ban on aid—but only if he certified to Congress that termination of assistance would have a serious adverse effect on vital U.S. interests and that he had received reliable assurances that the country in question would neither acquire or develop nuclear weapons nor assist other nations in doing so. Satisfaction of the first waiver condition was not difficult under the circumstances, but the administration was unable to certify that Pakistan had renounced nuclear weapons. Despite General Zia's insistence that his country's nuclear program was entirely peaceful, intelligence reports leaked to the press indicated that Pakistan was continuing its active efforts to develop nuclear explosives. Hence, no aid could be provided without a change in the Symington amendment.

This, and more, the Reagan administration began to seek in early April 1981. Instead of asking for a minimal amendment to existing law, one that would have merely allowed Pakistan to receive the proposed six-year aid package, the administration ambitiously hoped to rewrite the proviso so that the president could waive the aid embargo indefinitely—and not only for Pakistan but for any country he wished. The administration was using the pretext of the Pakistan situation to transform a law whose cutoff terms were unusually stringent into one that could be easily circumvented.

In successive steps the Republican-controlled Senate rolled back the administration's planned advances. In mid-May the Foreign Relations Committee approved an amendment to the fiscal year 1982 foreign aid authorization bill that effectively permitted the president to waive indefinitely the Symington amendment's prohibition on assistance, although only for Pakistan. When the whole Senate considered the bill on 21 October, Glenn argued for a substitute amendment that retained the original wording of the Symington amendment but granted Pakistan a one-time, six-year exemption to permit the administration's aid package to go forward. Support for Glenn's amendment was so strong that it was accepted by voice vote. In addition, despite strong administration opposition, Glenn won a close (51-45) vote on an amendment he had previously lost in committee, precluding the president from using the waiver provision in Section 670 of the Foreign Assistance Act—a provision prohibiting assistance to any non-nuclear-weapon state detonating a nuclear explosive—in the event of nuclear tests by either India or

Pakistan. Passage of a subsequent amendment by conservative Republican Senator Jesse Helms extended this limitation on the president's authority to include detonations by any nation. Thus, the Republican-controlled Senate not only had rolled back the Reagan administration's effort to weaken the Symington amendment across the board but also had strengthened related provisions of the Foreign Assistance Act at the expense of presidential discretion and directly contrary to the president's policy of seeking relaxation of stringent nonproliferation statutes.

By playing on fears that a mandatory aid cutoff for non-nuclear-weapon states detonating a nuclear device might preclude United States aid to Israel at a critical moment, the administration won somewhat greater flexibility in the version of the bill passed in the Democrat-controlled House on 9 December. But the final text of the bill, negotiated in a House-Senate conference six days later by Representatives Stephen Solarz and Jonathan Bingham and Senator John Glenn, went decidedly against the administration. The final version kept the Symington amendment intact and exempted only Pakistan for six years. Taking language from the House-passed bill, it also expanded Section 670 to provide that aid would be cut off to any non-nuclear-weapon state that detonated a nuclear device or received or transferred such a device. Where the original text of Section 670 had given the president generous leeway for waiving aid cutoffs, the conference version made the aid cutoff automatic. The president could, however, continue assistance for thirty days of congressional session if this was essential to the national interest; after that, aid could continue only if expressly authorized by Congress in a joint resolution. Several weeks later, a State Department official admitted privately to congressional staff that the vote on Pakistan convinced many administration officials of the futility of seeking amendments to the NNPA.

Meanwhile, yet another major setback was shaping up for the Reagan administration—this one engineered by Democratic Senator Gary Hart and Republican Senator Alan Simpson. The confrontation began brewing in mid-September 1981, when word slipped into the press that the administration intended to purchase plutonium produced by civilian nuclear power plants and use it in the expanding U.S. nuclear weapons program.[9] These reports worried not only legislators concerned about nuclear proliferation but also the U.S. nuclear industry and the nuclear industries of Western nations having advanced nuclear power programs. Behind this unusual alliance on a matter of nuclear power was the fact that the administration's proposal would have broken down the conceptual barrier, gradually built over the years, separating civilian and military uses of nuclear technology. The barrier had been crucial in helping to legitimize domestic nuclear power programs and nuclear power exports as strictly peaceful activities divorced from nuclear armaments.

Shortly after these press reports, Hart and Simpson drafted an amendment to the pending Nuclear Regulatory Commission Authorization bill prohibiting the use of plutonium from U.S. civilian power plants to make nuclear arms. Although the Reagan administration had never formally proposed the civilian-plutonium-for-weapons alternative to Congress, it strongly opposed the Hart-Simpson measure on the grounds that it was an unwarranted restriction on the executive branch's flexibility in meeting U.S. defense needs. Nevertheless, on 30 March 1982, when the prohibition came up for a dramatic vote on the Senate floor, it passed 88 to 9. Deeply concerned even about the possibility that a key premise of nuclear nonproliferation policy might be altered, the Senate had acted preemptively to stop the administration, notwithstanding concerns that this might marginally affect deployment of new U.S. nuclear arms. After a brief discussion, the House accepted the amendment in conference. The bill was ratified by both houses in December 1982, when an effort in the House to delete the ban on military uses of civilian plutonium was decisively beaten. The Republican-controlled Senate's overwhelming vote in March 1982 undoubtedly contributed to the administration's May 1982 decision to abandon its plans for weakening amendments to the NNPA.

Circumventing Legislation

Little more than eighteen months from the date it was formulated, the Reagan administration's legislative campaign for dramatically revising discretionary authority under the NNPA was its only alternative in pursuing its nuclear policy objectives. But while it exercised this option with some success, strenuous congressional opposition ultimately forced it to change course and actually move toward tighter nonproliferation controls.

As noted, one of the principal legislative objectives of the Reagan nonproliferation transition team had been elimination of the NNPA's retroactive export criterion prohibiting U.S. nuclear fuel and reactor shipments to any nation not accepting full-scope inspections. Although this legislative initiative failed, Reagan officials repeatedly sought to circumvent the NNPA's full-scope inspection requirement. In three instances—involving Brazil, South Africa, and India, none of which accepts comprehensive IAEA inspections—the administration encouraged other suppliers to step in and supply fuel, effectively short-circuiting the NNPA's embargo.

The administration did this for Brazil with an October 1981 announcement that the administration would not enforce a clause in a nuclear contract allowing the United States to demand millions of dollars in penalties if Brazil purchased fuel from a non-U.S. source. At the same time, the administration undercut the U.S. embargo on nuclear fuel exports to South Africa when it acquiesced in a U.S. nuclear broker's obtaining bulk uranium fuel for South Africa from European sources. Although subsequent testimony before a

House subcommittee suggested the administration had advance knowledge of the deal, the administration had not intervened to discourage the company from circumventing the embargo. Nor, according to State Department sources, did it express concern to the French government when that government agreed to fabricate the fuel into fuel rods for South Africa's Koeburg power reactors.

As for India, the administration worked out a deal in mid-1982 under which France would sell nuclear fuel to India. (The requirement in the United States-Indian agreement on nuclear cooperation that India purchase its materials exclusively from the United States was waived.) The administration was able to argue, with some merit, that this arrangement would help ensure that safeguards on the U.S.-built Tarapur reactors would be preserved. Nonetheless, when seen in conjunction with the administration's circumvention of embargoes on nuclear fuel sales to Brazil and South Africa, the deal appeared to be part of a larger effort to undermine the retroactive, full-scope inspection requirement of the NNPA.

At the same time that the administration sought to circumvent the NNPA embargoes, it was taking advantage of NNPA loopholes that permitted the export of nuclear components and commodities other than fuel and reactors to nations with uninspected nuclear facilities. In May 1981, for example, it authorized the export of computer process controls for use in an Argentine nuclear facility. Similarly, in April 1982, Secretary of Commerce Malcolm Baldrige wrote to Senator Charles Percy, chairman of the Subcommittee on Energy, Nuclear Proliferation and Governmental Processes, that while the administration would honor the NNPA embargo on fuel and reactor exports to South Africa, it had adopted ''a more flexible policy with respect to approvals of dual-use commodities and other materials and equipment which have nuclear-related uses.[10] Under this policy, the administration seemed ready to approve South African export requests for helium-3 (an element needed to conduct experiments on fuel quality, but usable in the production of tritium) as well as for a hot isostatic press (potentially useful for shaping the cores of nuclear explosives).

Congressional nonproliferation leaders intensely criticized these administration initiatives on the grounds that they undercut the NNPA's embargo of major nuclear exports. That criticism apparently had an impact on administration decision making. There is evidence, for example, that the administration stopped a deal in late 1982 under which European purchasers would buy South African-owned fuel currently stored in the United States. Under the arrangement, South Africa planned to use the proceeds to buy European-origin fuel for subsequent export to South Africa. Similarly, as a result of Percy's opposition, the proposed export of helium-3 and a hot isostatic press to South Africa was held up, and the goods may never be delivered.

Congressional opposition to executive branch sidestepping of the NNPA was carried furthest during the 97th Congress, in response to the administration's so-called plutonium policy. The preliminary formulation was announced as an initiative in the transition team report, then reiterated in the president's July 1981 statement, in which he said the United States would not inhibit reprocessing activities by key allies. At first, the administration implemented this policy by liberalizing case-by-case approval of requests to reprocess U.S.-origin spent fuel. By early 1982, the policy had been elaborated to include a proposal for granting blanket approvals of up to thirty years for the reprocessing of such spent fuel by Japan and members of the European Community. In addition, the policy would permit the export to these nations of long-embargoed reprocessing technology.

If implemented, this new policy would constitute a sea change in U.S. nuclear export policy. In the recent past, the United States has permitted reprocessing approvals only on a case-by-case basis. Recent administrations, both Republican and Democrat, have sought to discourage reprocessing technology because of the inherent risk of proliferation that comes with the separation of plutonium from spent reactor fuel. Presidents Ford and Carter not only ruled out the export of reprocessing technology but also imposed a moratorium on commercial reprocessing at home. The NNPA, moreover, had for the first time established criteria for approving reprocessing requests; they could be authorized only if they would not result in a "significant increase in the risk of proliferation," with "foremost consideration" to be given to whether the United States would have "timely warning" of a diversion of plutonium. The NNPA also established a process for public notice and fifteen-day congressional review for each approval. With the administration's one-time, thirty-year authorization, the opportunity for ongoing public and congressional scrutiny would be lost.

Members of Congress responsible for nuclear nonproliferation legislation quickly expressed concern over the administration's plutonium policy. They stated, among other things, that long-term or programmatic approvals for the reprocessing of U.S.-origin spent fuel are not permitted under the NNPA. How, they asked, for example, could proliferation risk be assessed thirty years in advance? The administration assured Congress it would have a chance to review the plutonium policy because it was to be implemented through new agreements with Japan and European nations for nuclear cooperation, at the time subject to congressional veto by concurrent resolution.

Congressional concern over this new policy was so great that legislators sought to challenge it preemptively, without waiting for the administration to present the new cooperative agreements. In early 1982, Representative Bingham had decided to introduce amendments to the NNPA. These were meant to initiate a discussion on how to prevent circumvention of the act—for example, by prohibiting export of nuclear commodities and components to nations with uninspected nuclear facilities. There was no intention of conducting hearings, for this might provide an opening for the administration to pursue its own legislative changes. But with the announcement of Reagan's plutonium policy, and mounting evidence that the administration had little support for its program, Bingham became sufficiently concerned and confident to hold hearings. In late summer, he decided not only to pursue the legislation but to strengthen it with the express purpose of stopping the administration's plutonium initiative. His provisions included an outright ban on the export of reprocessing technology, and stipulated that long-term permission to reprocess U.S.-supplied spent fuel would be granted only if the receiving country adopted the U.S. policy of limiting nuclear exports to countries accepting full-scope inspections.

Bingham's decision to hold hearings on his bill led to the unanimous passage of the legislation by the House Subcommittee on International Economic Policy and Trade, which he chaired in September 1982. In December, just before the 97th Congress adjourned, the full Foreign Affairs Committee passed the bill, by which time it had gained more than fifty cosponsors and had been introduced in the Senate. Thus, by the end of the first two years of the Reagan administration, the roles of Congress and the executive branch in regard to nuclear nonproliferation policy had reversed: the administration was trying to avoid changes in the NNPA; Congress was plotting a strategy to strengthen the act and further constrain executive action.

Epilogue: The 98th Congress

The pattern of legislative-executive branch tension over nuclear nonproliferation policy persisted in the 98th Congress. In June 1983, Secretary of State George Shultz promised Indian Prime Minister Indira Gandhi that the United States would shortly approve the export of spare parts for the Tarapur reactors. His pledge came in the wake of a *Washington Post* report that administration officials believed India was preparing for a second nuclear test and set off a storm of congressional criticism.[11] Within a week, fifty-two members of Congress had signed a letter to the president condemning the sale. In early August, nonbinding resolutions opposing the exports were introduced in both chambers.[12] Apparently as a result of this opposition, the proposed exports were still pending in mid-1984.

Barely a month after the Shultz visit, the Department of Energy approved West Germany's request to transfer 143 tons of heavy water to Argentina's two operating power reactors, with the remainder to be held in reserve for use in a third power reactor still under construction. The U.S. right to approve the transfer arose from the fact that the United States had originally supplied the material to West Germany for use in demonstration reactors there. Because heavy water is technically a nuclear "component," Argentine acceptance of full-scope safeguards was not a legal requirement for U.S. approval. Once again, congressional critics attacked the administration for undercutting the spirit of the NNPA, which seeks to withhold nuclear exports to countries until they accept full-scope safeguards.

The Indian and Argentine transfers spurred congressional interest in tightening the NNPA's export criteria to eliminate the inconsistent treatment in the law between fuel and reactors (whose export to nations refusing full-scope safeguards was prohibited) and components, technology, and so-called dual-use items (whose transfer to such countries was allowed). Taking advantage of legislation to reauthorize the Export Administration Act, governing licensing of all nonnuclear exports, Democratic Representative Howard Wolpe and Republican Senators Gordon Humphrey and William Roth introduced nonproliferation riders. The Wolpe amendment to the House version of the legislation (H.R. 2321), making acceptance by the recipient country of full-scope safeguards a condition for the export and retransfer of U.S.-origin nuclear components, technology, and dual-use items, passed the House in late September by a close vote, 196 to 189.[13] The Humphrey-Roth amendment to the Senate bill (S. 979), which did not cover dual-use items, passed the Senate unanimously in late February 1984, after an administration substitute was defeated by a 55-38 vote.[14] Both amendments permit the president to waive their export prohibitions if blocking an export would be "seriously prejudicial to the national security of the United States."

The Senate bill also contained an amendment by Senator William Proxmire, passed by a vote of 74-16, which provided that no new agreement for nuclear cooperation could become effective unless Congress approved it by a law or joint resolution.[15] That restored congressional authority jeopardized by the June 1983 Supreme Court decision that held unconstitutional provisions that allowed Congress to reverse executive branch actions by a majority vote in each body.[16] The first target of the Proxmire amendment was a controversial nuclear trade agreement the administration was about to sign with the People's Republic of China.

At this writing, the Export Administration Act extension remains tied up in a House-Senate conference, although there is no doubt that if the conferees reach agreement before the 98th Congress ends that act will contain a number of tough nonproliferation provisions. Negotiations on the United States-China accord were apparently completed in April 1984, and the agreement was initialed during Reagan's trip that month to Peking. It has not yet been forwarded to Capitol Hill and will not go into effect during this Congress.

Meanwhile, Congress took little action on the central provision of the Bingham bill, which had been reintroduced in both House and Senate even though Bingham had retired. The provision would curtail the administration's plutonium-use policy, including its proposal for the long-term approvals of reprocessing of U.S.-origin spent fuel. Throughout 1983, the administration did not appear to be actively pursuing this initiative; it seemed that negotiations with the Japanese, in particular, had bogged down. In late January 1984, the administration submitted two renegotiated agreements for cooperation to Congress, one with Sweden and the other with Norway, that contained long-term reprocessing approvals. Although Congress no longer possessed the authority to reject the accords by a two-house vote, the NNPA's requirement that agreements be subject to congressional review for sixty days of congressional session was still valid. Because of the impeccable nonproliferation credentials of the two nations involved and the absence of a statutory mechanism for blocking the accords, the precedent-setting reprocessing provisions of the two agreements raised little interest except among the handful of legislators who appreciated their importance. In mid-May 1984, Congressmen Howard Wolpe and Michael Barnes and Senator Alan Cranston, along with several critizen action groups, filed suit in federal court to have the agreements declared invalid on the grounds that they contained an illegal interpretation of the NNPA's reprocessing approval standards.

As this piece was written before the 1984 presidential election, it was not possible to declare a clear winner in the battle over the administration's nonproliferation policy agenda. India, Brazil, and South Africa have received fuel for their reactors, and Argentina's purchase of heavy water from West Germany has been approved, despite strong congressional opposition; on the other hand, proposed component exports to South Africa and India are still pending. In fights over nonproliferation legislation, congressional critics have made few concessions and remain on the offensive. What is perhaps clearest is that Congress not only can have a say on nuclear policies proposed by the executive but can even have the final word.

Notes

1. James L. Malone to James Edwards (secretary-designate of energy), 18 December 1980, Tab C (authors' files).
2. U.S., Congress, Senate Committee on Governmental Affairs, Subcommittee on Energy, Nuclear Proliferation and Government Processes, *Hearing on Nuclear Nonproliferation Policy and the Implications of the New Technology*, 97th Cong., 1st sess., 19 November 1981, p. 8.
3. U.S., Congress, Senate, Committee on Governmental Affairs, Subcommittee on Energy, Nuclear Proliferation and Government Processes, *Hearing on U.S. Policy on Export of Helium-3 and Other Nuclear Materials and Technology*, 97th Cong., 1st sess., 13 May 1982, p. 49.
4. U.S., General Accounting Office, *The Nuclear Non-Proliferation Act of 1978 Should Be Selectively Modified*, OCG-81-2 (Washington, D.C.: GAO, 1981).
5. Senate Resolution 179 and House Resolution 177 (17 July 1981).

6. James L. Malone, "Memorandum to IG [Interagency Group] Members of the IG on U.S. Non-Proliferation and Peaceful Nuclear Cooperation Policy," 2 October 1981, p. 1 (authors' files).

7. *Washington Post*, 11 October 1981.

8. *Hearing on Nuclear Nonproliferation Policy and the Implications of the New Technology*, p. 33. (See note 2 above.)

9. *New York Times*, 11 September 1981.

10. Malcolm Baldrige to Charles Percy, 12 May 1982.

11. *Washington Post*, 23 June 1983.

12. See, e.g., Senate Resolution 1981 (1983).

13. See *Congressional Record*, 30 September 1983, p. H7781.

14. See ibid., 28 February 1984, p. S1850.

15. S. 979, sec. 27 (1983).

16. *Immigration and Naturalization Service* v. *Chadha*, 103 S. Ct. 2764 (1983).

7

The Nuclear Marketplace and the Nonproliferation Regime

Edward F. Wonder

The development and acceptance of the international nonproliferation regime has been one of the most remarkable achievements of the postwar era. The nonproliferation regime has developed incrementally over time, often in spite of the inability of the two superpowers to come to grips with their own arms race. States otherwise zealous to protect their sovereignty have accepted international constraints on that same sovereignty where nuclear power is concerned. A complicated (and fragile) multitier structure of bilateral undertakings, regional compacts, and multilateral and international understandings and formal treaty obligations and institutions is now in place. The architects of this regime can rightfully point to it with pride, but pride in past achievements will be of little help in the next twenty years as that regime is assaulted from a number of directions.

As the principal architect and defender of the regime, it is the United States, with its global interests and responsibilities, that stands most to reap the benefits and bear the costs of upholding this regime. The stability of a regime depends, in part, on the existence of a dominant actor that is able to enforce adherence to its rules and absorb what might be a disproportionate share of the costs of upholding the regime. The United States has played this role in the regime. Its nonproliferation posture was marked by a constancy and consistency for almost two and a half decades, during which a remarkable bipartisan consensus existed in nonproliferation policy. But since the mid-1970s this has not been the case. Not only have successive administrations taken different approaches (although there is a tendency for the supporters of one administra-

Written and submitted in May 1984, when employed as a senior consultant with International Energy Associates, Ltd. The views expressed are those of the author and not of the International Energy Associates.

tion to exaggerate the "deviations" of another in this highly politicized issue area) but the intrusion of Congress into the making of foreign policy has been particularly marked in nonproliferation. As a result, the executive branch has to negotiate at two levels: with foreign governments, and with (implicitly) Congress.

Whether the United States still can play the role of protector is open to question. Even more serious is whether the regime, as now constituted, can stand up to a multitude of pressures while the position of its dominant actor erodes.

Mounting Pressure on the Foundation

The nonproliferation regime rests on a number of pillars. First, Soviet-U.S. consensus on the risks posed by proliferation has helped propel the regime forward at critical junctures, most notably in the events leading to the conclusion of the Nonproliferation Treaty (NPT) in 1968. Second, early U.S. domination of international nuclear markets was critical to the advancement of international safeguards and peaceful use undertakings and to broadening participation in the NPT and International Atomic Energy Agency (IAEA). To these two pillars must be added a third: leverage over the proliferation problem countries. The countries of main proliferation concern in the initial decade and a half of the regime possessed the technical prerequisites for nuclear weapons but found their potential political or security motives effectively addressed by bilateral or multilateral security measures and diplomatic relationships. Even then, the record was mixed, in that proliferation occurred in France and China but not the Federal Republic of Germany, Japan, and other industrial states. Finally, the regime has required a degree of mutual trust and consensus for the diverse (and potentially antithetical) interests of its adherents to be held together. Each of these four pillars is now subject to cross pressures that could pull down one or more of them.

Despite their unresolved and serious differences over strategic arms control issues, the Soviet Union and the United States have maintained consensus that proliferation would damage the security interests of both countries. Both recognized that proliferation could severely complicate both arms-race stability and crisis stability. The oft-cited specter of catalytic war—the potential for a regional nuclear war, say in South Asia, to draw in the superpowers—is only one problem of crisis stability. At the least, proliferation could impose new weapons requirements and complicate strategic planning, making arms-race stability all the more elusive. One need only to recall the uncertainties created by the Chinese nuclear buildup in the 1960s, and the weapons-planning responses of both the Soviets and the United States, to see this latter process at work.

Keeping nuclear weapons out of the hands of states on the periphery of the Soviet Union has been the primary objective of Soviet nonproliferation policy. With the exception of the PRC, that objective has been achieved. Both Japan's and West Germany's nonnuclear status have been cemented in the NPT, as has that of Yugoslavia, which was never a real threat. Thus, the nuclear-weapon status of the Soviet flank has largely been determined, with the potential exception of the Near East, where proliferation could have untold consequences. At the same time, the rationale for a Soviet commitment to nonproliferation beyond its flank merits examination. Although there have been recent indications of a resurgence of Soviet concern for nonproliferation, one must consider whether Soviet nonproliferation efforts will be conditioned by geopolitical calculations (and certainly a desire to avoid any blame for contributing to proliferation anywhere), such that proliferation occurring far afield from the Soviet Union might be viewed as a largely U.S. problem potentially working in the Soviet interest if U.S. resources are tied down to prevent it. As a result, while Soviet cooperation in stopping proliferation might presumably be forthcoming where particular problem states or volatile regions are involved, the burden of maintaining the commitment to nonproliferation as a principle and shoring up the obstacles to proliferation in many regions will fall squarely on the United States.

The second pillar—the international market structure—has changed markedly from the period when many of the elements of the regime were put in place.[1] This change has occurred at four levels: the balance of power in reactor export markets; fuel supply; the economic and political characteristics of the nuclear export markets; and the identity of equipment and technology suppliers.

The declining U.S. share of the reactor export market has been marked, but it really should not be such a great surprise. The same technology licensing agreements that helped U.S. reactor vendors penetrate European and Japanese markets have provided a technical basis for the reactor market to become much more competitive. Figure 7.1 demonstrates vividly the slide in U.S. domination of reactor export markets.

What we have witnessed is an inevitable maturation process in the reactor industries of other advanced industrial states. Greater competitiveness was a natural consequence of this process, which has paralleled that of other technology-intensive industries.

The U.S. loss of market share is equally pronounced in the enrichment market, with even greater consequence, for it was believed early on that fuel supply, even more than the transfer of technology, would be the principal vehicle by which the United States could extend the reach of nonproliferation measures. Until 1970, when the Soviet Union first sold enrichment services to a West German utility, the United States held a complete monopoly on the

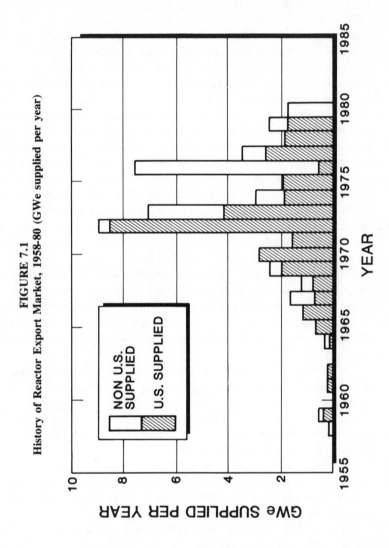

FIGURE 7.1

History of Reactor Export Market, 1958-80 (GWe supplied per year)

TABLE 7.1
Suppliers to the International Commercial Nuclear Market

	UNITED STATES	AUSTRALIA	ARGENTINA	BELGIUM	BRAZIL	CANADA	CHINA	FRANCE	GERMANY (FRG)	INDIA	ITALY	JAPAN	KOREA	SOUTH AFRICA	SPAIN	SWEDEN	SWITZERLAND	USSR	U.K.	NETHERLANDS
COMPLETE REACTORS	x				x		x	x			x	x				x	x	x		
MAJOR REACTOR COMPONENTS	x		x	x	x	x	x	x	x	x	x	x			x	x	x	x	x	
DESIGN/ENGINEERING	x		x	x	x	x	x	x	x	x	x	x			x		x	x	x	
FUEL FABRICATION	x		x	x	x	x	x	x	x	x	x	x			x	x				
URANIUM	x	x			x	x	x	x					x	x						
URANIUM PROCESSING	x				x	x	x	x		x	x	x	x				x	x		
URANIUM ENRICHMENT	x	●				x	x	x	●	●	●	●	●	x			x	x	x	
REPROCESSING	●				●		x	●	●	x	●	●					x	x	x	

x = Regularly offers commodity or service in commercial export market

* = Has technical capability but has not yet made commercial offering

international commercial enrichment market. By 1984, the U.S. share had slid to around 35 percent. In the interim, two European enrichment consortia had come into existence, one of which had set up a new entity with Australian interests to build a plant in Australia at some date, and Japan had initiated its own enrichment program aimed at displacing foreign suppliers from part of its market. Although some in the United States have argued that a more far-sighted U.S. policy in the early 1970s could have headed off these developments, in retrospect they appear as an inevitable concomitant of the maturation of nuclear industries.

While the contraction of projected nuclear growth has received wide attention, there has also been a marked change in the composition of nuclear export markets that could be just as important, particularly for nonproliferation. The advanced industrial states that constituted the bulk of the reactor export market in the 1960s are, by and large, now self-sufficient and closed off to foreign vendors. Export opportunities will, in the future, be confined to technically less self-sufficient industrial countries, such as Italy and Belgium, where there is still some dependence on foreign technology and engineering services, and to less advanced countries, with the size of the market for outside technology, engineering, and hardware increasing in inverse proportion to the level of technological infrastructure in the customer state.

This shift will have several consequences. First, it appears that not only will the number of customers be few but opportunties for full-station sales will be extremely limited. Thus, exports will not provide the same loading on vendor industrial facilities as would a domestic sale. Second, the prominence of economically weaker states in the export market means that export prospects will be less secure and much more sensitive to such factors as the availability of foreign exchange and lender confidence in customer-state economies. Third, several so-called problem countries figure prominently in the market, making the political complexion of the market different from that of the past.

Finally, the structure of the nuclear supply sector is more complex. In addition to the established suppliers of reactor systems and commercial fuel-cycle services, there are emerging suppliers capable of supplying components, research reactors, engineering services, and, in the future, possibly sensitive fuel-cycle technology. Table 7-1 delineates the current supply structure. Even if these new suppliers are competitive on neither cost nor technology grounds, they could penetrate markets by exploiting regional political affinities and, if their own nonproliferation requirements are less onerous, discontent with the discriminatory aspect of the nonproliferation regime or industrial state hegemony.

The political consequences of these industrial developments have been several, none of them favorable to U.S. interests. Direct U.S. leverage based on supply relationships has declined. Surplus enrichment and reactor supply capacity enable customer states to diversify their supply relationships. The behavior of the enrichment market in particular, with a highly active secondary market and substantial surplus production capacity, appears to erode any basis for obtaining nonproliferation "leverage" via fuel supply. No self-respecting customer state need allow itself to become overly dependent on any single supplier of fuel or reactors. Thus, old arguments about gaining leverage via supply, which might have been valid when the United States monopolized the enrichment market, are less credible now. If anything, it might be the suppliers who become dependent on staying in the good graces of their customers.

The emergence of a supply structure differentiated not only by the cost or technological competitiveness of its players but also by their nonproliferation conditions has made the issue of supplier cooperation even more imperative. However, the zero-sum nature of the competition in a small market, which could shrink even more, discourages such cooperation. This problem might become worse as more suppliers come into the picture, if the functioning of the market becomes even more politically conditioned. Finally, the political coloration of the prospective customers makes dealing with such issues as differential treatment for NPT and non-NPT parties unavoidable.

The status of the third pillar of the regime is even more alarming. Unlike the 1950s and 1960s, there might be less overt leverage over the potential proliferators, with the notable exceptions of South Korea and Taiwan. In the case of Pakistan, arms sales and other security assurances have neither stopped work on fuel-cycle facilities nor yet brought them under safeguards. Intelligence gaps have been dismaying, as witnessed by Pakistan's ability to procure centrifuge technology and equipment and elude detection until it was too late to block that project, as well as by Argentina's surprise announcement at the end of 1983 that it had achieved a gaseous diffusion capability. While the critics of restraints based on the civilian fuel cycle have loudly argued that diplomatic and security-related confidence-building measures will be much more effective for the "real" proliferation threats, it is not clear, given the tremendous diversity of situations one encounters in looking at the current problem countries, just what the right "formula" is or even if there is one at all.

Finally, the fourth pillar—mutual trust—has emerged battered from the 1970s. There are unresolved differences between suppliers and customers over how the basic bargain of the NPT—nonproliferation undertakings in exchange for full access to nuclear cooperation and exports of nuclear materials, equipment, and technology—is to be interpreted. This tension was already apparent in the mid-1970s, by which time serious reassessments of supply policies were underway in several supplier states, not just the United States. To this was added an emerging debate over fuel-cycle policies and the role to be played by plutonium, which would divide the ranks of the supplier states. The Carter administration's more restrictive nuclear export policy and the passage of the Nuclear Nonproliferation Act (NNPA) in 1978 clearly contributed to an "erosion of confidence" in nuclear supply relationships, but it is unfair to assign all of the blame to these two factors. The tensions were already present in the regime, and, in this author's view, conflict among suppliers and between suppliers and customers over highly charged issues, such as the transfer of sensitive fuel-cycle technology, was inevitable.

Continued finger-pointing at the Carter policy and the NNPA currently serves little purpose. The damage is done, and the politico-legal environment in which U.S. nuclear export policy must be conducted is not going to become any more permissive, given congressional activism on nonproliferation and attempts to pass even more restrictive legislation.

Issues and Approaches

The working of the nuclear marketplace suggests that maintaining the nonproliferation regime in the years to come will require us to achieve greater supplier cooperation; to adapt the regime to new supply sources and marketing arrangements; to uphold the legitimacy of the NPT in dealing with countries standing outside the NPT; and to strengthen sanctions against violations of nonproliferation undertakings and principles. Neither these policy prescriptions nor the issues that they raise fall into neat, self-contained categories. The overlap will be apparent, but each has unique features that merit separate comment.

While supplier consensus on stiffer nonproliferation controls has been a prominent objective of U.S. policy, the prospective industrial dynamics do not bode well for achieving this objective. The export market will be small, and, as indicated, competition nearly approximates a zero-sum game. Recent speculation on the potential for small and medium-sized reactors to open up new markets otherwise uninterested in reactors of a thousand megawatts or greater overlooks the time required to prove and commercialize new designs and the ability of various institutional obstacles to retard or even block their development. Moreover, the receptivity of the market for such designs remains undemonstrated. Consequently, the reactor export market will likely remain limited to countries having, for starters, fairly sizeable electricity grids capable of accommodating larger reactors. Further, the entry of new suppliers, especially if they enjoy political advantages, could make competition even more intense and further discourage adoption of stiffer nonproliferation conditions.

Beyond these factors, it must be acknowledged that nonproliferation has represented a "free good" for the other suppliers, and that they have been able to "exploit" the U.S. commitment to maintaining the nonproliferation regime. The situation is not all that unlike that found in the "burden-sharing" issue of the Western alliance, where strategic security is a public good available to all the alliance members while the United States shoulders a disproportionate share of the cost of providing this security. As in the case of military stability, the ability and willingness of the United States to uphold the nonproliferation system is of key importance. It is not immediately apparent that the non-U.S. suppliers, with some major exceptions, have demonstrated a commitment to nonproliferation consistent with their economic interest in nuclear trade. A zero-sum competition for reactor exports hardly offers incentives to rectify this situation.

The source of continued policy differences is not simply concern for the health of an export-dependent industry (and, given the size of the prospective export market, it is probably misleading to expect exports to provide anything more than a very temporary bridge for reactor industries until domestic markets revive, if ever). Rather, the differences are deeply rooted in contrasting political structures, in which the U.S. situation stands out for the lack of industry influence over government policy; contrasting views of the potential "strategic" uses of nuclear trade as a way to open up spheres of industrial influence in industrializing customer states; and, it seems, ambivalent views in some supplier states of the importance of nonproliferation, or, at least, an unwillingness to accept any costs in promoting nonproliferation. In its most extreme form, one encounters the perspective that the commercial spread of nuclear technology bears no relationship to the risk of proliferation. Thus, the problem is not simply the insufficiency of export prospects to satisfy all suppliers, and the solution is not one of a reactor cartel or some other such formulation. The roots go far deeper, the clash of underlying perspectives is not unique to the nonproliferation issue, and the rift may well defy solution.

This is not to deny that progress has been made. More components, especially those related to centrifuge enrichment plants, have been added to the "trigger" list of the Nuclear Suppliers Group (NSG). More attention is being paid to strengthening intelligence related to efforts by would-be proliferators to obtain sensitive facilities piece by piece. However, the suppliers are still apart on adopting tougher, uniformly applied export criteria, such as full-scope safeguards. Mutual restraint in dealing with the most egregious proliferators, such as Pakistan, is vulnerable to the first supplier to break ranks. The search for far-reaching supplier consensus could, in the end, prove to be a search for a modern-day Holy Grail—tantalizingly on the horizon but a phantom nonetheless. Thus, one must ask whether the United States must lower its sights a bit, especially with respect to insisting that other suppliers formally adopt full-scope safeguards as an export criterion.

Closely related to the issue of supplier cooperation is the problem of how to deal with new suppliers and supply arrangements. This problem has two parts: one related to the new, emerging suppliers capable of supplying perhaps research reactors and a limited range of technology; the other related to the potential for new technical alliances between existing vendors to create new marketing arrangements. Of the two, the former will be the most difficult one with which to deal, as some of the potential new suppliers reject the nonproliferation regime as discriminatory and refuse to accept full-scope safeguards on their own programs. It is here that the Reagan administration's controversial "dialogue" strategy with states that do not accept safeguards on all of their nuclear activities is relevant. This strategy not only must succeed in persuading these countries to accept full-scope safeguards for themselves but must also persuade them to tighten up their own nuclear export policies. Anything less could discredit the approach with a Congress already disposed against it.

Some progress has been made. South Africa announced in January of 1984 that it will adhere to the NSG guidelines in its export policy, while still rejecting full-scope safeguards for itself. The PRC has stated it will require IAEA safeguards and a peaceful-use pledge for its nuclear exports. However, moving the new suppliers beyond this stage to more comprehensive requirements will be more difficult, especially because some of them will have been on the receiving end of tougher nonproliferation policies, primarily those of the United States. There thus appears to be an unavoidable tension between U.S. objectives in regard to supplier cooperation and the need to integrate new suppliers into a nonproliferation system that they view as discriminatory.

The second part of the new supplier problem is potentially more tractable. The technical alliances that appear to be playing important roles in efforts of vendors to position themselves to offer better products and to remain at the forefront of technology will likely create new marketing arrangements as well. There will undoubtedly be temptations to try to export from the partner facing the least onerous home government export controls. Thus, technical alliances appear to create an additional need to coordinate supplier policies if we are to avoid the inevitable conflicts that could result from an export strategy that follows a "course of least resistance."

Despite the evidence that a multilateral approach on controls might be essential, however, Congress has recently demonstrated an alarming tendency to become preoccupied with the minutiae of unilateral "leverage," seeking to close minor "loopholes" in the NNPA in the misbegotten belief that this would somehow bring other countries to heel. All this would really do is leave the other suppliers, whose cooperation the United States must continue to seek, scratching their heads in wonderment.

Closely related to the above is a third cluster of issues having to do with whether NPT parties should be treated differently than non-NPT countries. Some have argued since the NPT was implemented that NPT parties should, and must, be given freer access to technology (or at the least should benefit from some sort of positive discrimination vis-à-vis nonparties) if the legitimacy of the NPT is to be upheld. Indeed, some non-nuclear-weapon countries, in acceding to Article III of the treaty, argued that Article IV should be interpreted as entitling them to the widest possible access to technology. The United States has rejected this position, and, upon inspection of the credentials of all the NPT parties, it is clear that treaty adherence alone does not provide a sufficient basis for differential treatment. And, clearly, the record demonstrates that actual policy practice has necessarily made finer distinctions among states. At the same time, the tension between upholding the NPT and discretion in dealings with individual cases remains.

The NPT has two major advantages: its universal applicability and the clarity of its safeguard undertakings. But as a common denominator approach, the NPT is not tailored to regional circumstances. This intimately affects the potential for proliferation, and might yet necessitate carefully tailored, region-specific measures that could either go beyond the NPT or at least be better synchronized with regional political dynamics. The persistence of the regional institutional theme, taking the form of fuel-cycle centers, inspection agencies, or treaty commitments, demonstrates the strength of the regional perspective.

Critics of the Reagan administration policy of "dialogue" with some sensitive states have charged that it undermines the NPT. That it obscures the NPT as a basis for discrimination is no doubt true, but it was never U.S. policy to refrain from dealing with nonparties. And, we must take care not to elevate the NPT to a level of importance that might be disproportionate to its real value. The NPT provides a valuable good: an open declaration of peaceful intent; forbearance of any nuclear explosives; and acceptance of full-scope safeguards. Achievement of this good is not necessarily confined to the NPT, however, and one can envision circumstances where the need for confidence building will require new or revamped regional measures. If dialogue leads to effective regional undertakings as a substitute for NPT adherence or as an adjunct to it, the result could actually be stronger bulwarks against proliferation.

The last issue to be dealt with here is perhaps the most important: sanctions. The Foreign Assistance Act and the Atomic Energy Act contain sanction provisions. The International Atomic Energy Agency's statute and the NPT contain a section on procedures to be followed in case of violation. Nevertheless, the focus of most nonproliferation thinking and policy has been on prevention. Less attention has been given to the complexities of what to do in case of violation; when to do it, and in collaboration with whom, if anyone, and even what the objectives in imposing sanctions should be.

Some experts have recently pointed out that proliferation is not a single, Rubicon-like event. Rather, it is a process in which a country's emergence as a credible nuclear power involves gradual development of effective delivery systems and assembly of sufficient quantities of nuclear weapons. One detonation does not a nuclear power make. Thus, proliferation is a continuous game offering a number of opportunities to stem the process before a credible nuclear arsenal is assembled. At the same time, the first detonation, or the threat thereof, can set off a chain reaction of events (such as preemptive military strikes against nuclear facilities) that can rapidly unravel regional stability. Therefore, sanctions applied after a detonation could come too late.

The sanctions issue is obviously tricky, and too much so to discuss any further here. But this issue deserves much more attention than it has received. If the foundation of the nonproliferation regime erodes, and other countries do not step in to uphold it if U.S. influence declines, we could well be faced with situations where sanctions are called for. Failure to look ahead now would leave us unprepared for that day.

The challenge to the nonproliferation regime, then, is both serious and multifaceted. There is no single or overriding source of that regime's problems, nor is there a single solution. Rolling back the NNPA and "letting the U.S. nuclear industry compete" make for a good slogan but will not change the seriousness of the nonproliferation challenge.

Note

1. See W. Walker and M. Lonnroth, *Nuclear Power Struggles: Industrial Competition and Proliferation Control* (London: Allen & Unwin, 1983).

8

Dealing with the Problem Countries

Rodney W. Jones

The test of America's policies to prevent nuclear proliferation is the so-called problem countries, those states that pose the greatest risk of "going nuclear." Most visible—and the source of greatest concern—are those countries which have developed or appear to be in the process of developing nuclear weapons capabilities. In addition to Pakistan, near-nuclear countries of note include India, Israel, South Africa, Argentina, South Korea, and Taiwan.

Several other countries, including Iraq, Iran, Libya, and Brazil, seem to pose proliferation risks in the longer term. More problematic are countries, such as Mexico, that, although they seem to represent little or no proliferation risk themselves, pose difficult problems by challenging restrictions in nuclear export policy. I will examine U.S. policy toward some of the problem countries, paying particular attention to Pakistan. The constants in U.S. policy and the few changes wrought by the Reagan administration will be noted throughout. Although the Reagan administration's attitude toward international nuclear policy is different in some respects from the Carter administration's, changes in the substance of that policy have not been as sharp or numerous as many observers expected.

What are the major differences between Reagan and Carter on nuclear policy? First of all, the Reagan administration is more outspoken in promoting nuclear energy, more candid about resuming U.S. technological leadership, and more eager to see American vendors profit from nuclear export opportunities—all matters on which the Carter administration was ambivalent. Second, while the present administration insists that its commitment to nonproliferation objectives is no less firm, it has adopted a somewhat different philosophy toward the problem. High priority is now given to restoring or reinforcing the reputation of the United States both as a reliable supplier of nuclear goods and services and as a predictable partner in nuclear cooperation. This reflects a belief that reliability reduces the incentives for proliferation and pre-empts national drives for nuclear independence that ultimately increase prolif-eration risks. Third, Reagan has adopted a less inhibited posture on spent-fuel reprocessing and fuel-cycle use of plutonium. These are now accepted as normal objectives in certain advanced countries where the use of nuclear energy is well established and seems to be suitable technically and econom-ically.

What is interesting about these Reagan policy differences is how little they apply to the countries most likely to proliferate. On specific issues, nuclear policy toward problem countries has hardly changed at all. In many cases, the principle of reliable supply has been overtaken by events, and the Reagan ad-ministration is no more permissive than its predecessor about reprocessing in the problem countries. With respect to these countries, however, there has been some innovation in the use of nonnuclear policy instruments for non-proliferation purposes. A significant difference of approach is apparent, for example, in the use of security assistance, conventional arms transfers, and other such instruments to enhance U.S. security commitments and revitalize security arrangements, thus reducing proliferation incentives. Arguably, this fresh approach has already proved to be of value for nonproliferation purposes in the cases of Taiwan and South Korea. Also, in contrast to the Carter ap-proach, the Reagan administration prefers to use the carrot more than the stick with respect to problem countries. Today this approach is epitomized in U.S. policy toward Pakistan, to which I shall return later.

Legislative Retroactivity

Certain provisions of the 1978 Nuclear Nonproliferation Act (NNPA) call for the suspension of U.S. nuclear exports to countries that fail to comply with new U.S. conditions. In cases such as India and Brazil, where these provi-sions have been applied retroactively, overriding previous U.S. export com-mitments, the NNPA embargoes have become serious irritants in bilateral re-lations. In mid-1982, the Reagan administration moved to set aside such a source of friction with India and, earlier, adopted a special waiver that tem-porarily eased similar difficulties with Brazil. The basic problem for the United States was that neither country was willing to accept "full-scope" safeguards, which the NNPA established as a new condition for continued U.S. nuclear exports. In both cases, the U.S. supply of nuclear fuel for power reactors was suspended.

Fuel resupply to the Tarapur power station, which had been built in India in the 1960s with U.S. assistance, had become a bilateral issue even before the NNPA, owing to intervenor challenges in hearings before the Nuclear Regulatory Commission (NRC). India's detonation in 1974 of what it described as a "peaceful nuclear device" attracted considerable attention and had more than a little to do with the passage of the NNPA four years later. Once the grace period provided for by the NNPA had expired, the act's requirements came into conflict with U.S. obligations under the 1963 cooperation agreement. In return for Indian acceptance of safeguards on Tarapur as well as U.S. "consent rights" over any reprocessing of spent fuel from Tarapur—over which rights the United States and India disagree—the 1963 agreement obligated the United States to provide the needed low-enriched uranium fuel for thirty years (i.e., until 1993), the presumed operating life of the Indian reactors. The agreement also required India to operate Tarapur exclusively on U.S.-origin fuel.

Initial U.S. efforts to persuade India to comply with the full-scope safeguards requirement produced a deadlock. Delhi declared that U.S. suspension of fuel supply would be illegal and tantamount to unilateral abrogation of the agreement. Such an act, India contended, would free Tarapur from the safeguards obligation, which was explicitly linked to the U.S. supply of reactor fuel. India, moreover, would in that case consider itself free to find an alternative source of fuel and to begin reprocessing spent fuel. India even made the claim that it could operate Tarapur on plutonium separated from U.S.-origin spent fuel.

President Carter, as permitted by the NNPA, issued an export license allowing one additional fuel shipment in order to buy time for further negotiation. (The license had been held up by the NRC partly because of concern over the duration of International Atomic Energy Agency safeguards on Tarapur.) The narrow margin by which Congress upheld the executive order seemed to be a clear message that a subsequent license application would not pass. While this served as a spur to negotiations, it was insufficient to break the deadlock until well into the Reagan administration.

Shortly before Prime Minister Indira Gandhi's state visit to the United States in July 1982, the basic elements for a resolution of the dispute finally fell into place. France would take over the supply of fuel for Tarapur, relieving the United States of this obligation, while India agreed to continue the safeguards already in force. IAEA (International Atomic Energy Agency) safeguards were applied to Tarapur under a 1969 trilateral agreement pursuant to the 1963 Tarapur cooperation agreement. Except for the substitution of French fuel supply, the original 1963 agreement also remains in force. What is still in dispute, however, is whether the United States thereby retains consent rights over the reprocessing of U.S.-origin spent fuel at Tarapur, as the United States claims. India argues that the United States has delegated the consent rights to the IAEA. While France was only too eager to inherit the role of supplier, it agreed with the U.S. position and urged India to accept the view that Tarapur safeguards should be applied "in perpetuity," rather than expire in 1993 along with the fuel-supply obligation. Since India appears to have resisted, the question of what will happen in 1993 is open.

At this point, though, an issue poisoning U.S.-Indian relations was set aside through practical compromise. Those who view the U.S. concession as a "caving in," or as a circumvention of the NNPA, may be overlooking the most important result: despite an act of unilateral withdrawal mandated by U.S. law, which otherwise might have jeopardized nonproliferation objectives, Washington succeeded in preserving the integrity of safeguards on a U.S.-origin nuclear facility and its associated spent fuel. In retrospect, it appears that a settlement became possible when the fuel on hand in India was approaching exhaustion and Delhi, confronted with the invasion of Afghanistan and changing domestic priorities, became willing to work toward improved relations with the United States rather than cause further deterioration of relations.

After the fuel substitution issue was settled, India raised the Tarapur question in a different light. India applied to the United States for supply of spare parts and instruments to repair power–plant components and remedy radiation problems that jeopardized the "health and safety" of operating personnel. Though not obligatory, such exports were permissible and formerly regarded as natural in the framework of the 1963 agreement. Had the agreement been abrogated, of course, it seems unlikely that the question would have been entertained. Even so, the transfer seemed to require a presidential waiver and congressional consent under the NNPA, Secretary of State Shultz announced on 30 June 1983, while visiting India, that the United States would support India's acquisition of the spare parts, preferably from third-party sources but possibly also through direct U.S. supply. Though a subsequent search for compatible parts and equipment has been underway in decommissioned West German and Italian facilities, the final solution seems to have been deferred, perhaps because of indications that India might resume nuclear explosive testing as well as revived congressional concern about possible circumventions of the NNPA.

The conflict with Brazil also arose from NNPA retroactivity, but in a different way, and without the intensity that characterized the Tarapur dispute. Still, it became an impediment to improving U.S. relations with the largest Latin American power. Although Brasília has signed and ratified the 1967 Tlatelolco Treaty, which provides for a nuclear-free zone in the region, it has not waived the treaty into force or accepted full-scope safeguards.

The issue in the Brazilian case had to do with fuel resupply for the Angra I reactor sold to Brazil by Westinghouse, for which U.S. fuel supply had previously been assumed. Owing to a series of technical difficulties, Angra I had not come into full operation on its original schedule. But in anticipation that it soon would, Brazil applied for a U.S. fuel export license at the time of Vice-President Bush's 1981 visit. Under the terms of the NNPA, Brazil by then could no longer be supplied with U.S. nuclear fuel. Pursuant to the U.S. Department of Energy's (DOE's) exclusive enrichment contract with Brazil, moreover, Brazil would have been required to pay millions of dollars in penalties if it sought enrichment services elsewhere. The penalties issue was an embarrassing catch-22 that served no useful nonproliferation purpose. Hence, the Reagan administration acted to waive the Energy Department penalties. This action did not remove the basic conflict between U.S. supply commitments and the requirements of the NNPA, but it did remove an unnecessary irritant in U.S.-Brazilian relations. It may also have improved the chances for Washington to engage Brasília in dialogue about the problem of new nuclear supplier countries that are not part of the Nuclear Suppliers Group.

Sensitive Technologies

Argentina has been regarded as a problem country for quite some time because of its military-administered nuclear program and its determination, like India, to develop reprocessing and a complete heavy water–natural uranium fuel cycle with indigenously built, sensitive facilities kept free from safeguards. Argentina is also a holdout from the Nonproliferation Treaty (NPT) and still hesitant on ratification of the Tlatelolco Treaty. U.S. nonproliferation efforts have focused on persuading Argentina to ratify Tlatelolco, if not the NPT, and to accept full-scope safeguards.

For the Carter administration, the active issue was to persuade Argentina to accept additional safeguards coverage in return for assistance with heavy water technology and a new reactor. Canada was prepared to offer such assistance but, like the United States, required full-scope safeguards as an export condition. To counter Argentina's tendency to play suppliers off against one another, West Germany was encouraged to adopt the same position, which it tentatively agreed to do. Argentina dropped its Canadian inquiries, however, and sought separate contracts with Swiss firms for heavy water technology and West German firms for the reactor. The Swiss declined to insist on full-scope safeguards for the sale of the heavy water plant, and West Germany then followed suit with the reactor contract. Consummation of this arrangement may enable Argentina not only to achieve independence in the heavy water fuel cycle but to keep indigenous, sensitive facilities free of safeguards.

Inheriting this situation, the Reagan administration found it had little or no "wiggle room" under the NNPA to pursue a nuclear supplier relationship with Argentina and correspondingly little leverage for nonproliferation purposes. The situation was compounded by the Falkland Islands conflict of 1982, which caused bilateral relations to plummet and—in the absence of political change through elections—might have sharply increased Argentina's incentives to develop nuclear weapons. Hence the Reagan administration sought greater administrative flexibility over nuclear-related exports within existing laws to preserve a relationship with Argentina.

Prior to the Falklands crisis, the Reagan administration approved export of a U.S. process control system to Switzerland for ultimate use at the Argentine heavy water plant. Initial consideration was also given at that time to retransfer of 143 tons of U.S.-origin heavy water from West Germany to Argentina for power plant use. Deferred until after the Falklands conflict, this retransfer eventually was approved, in August 1983, by the U.S. Department of Energy.

Controversy over the DOE approval procedure, which omitted consultation with the Nuclear Regulatory Commission, together with questions about proposed exports to India and South Africa, stimulated congressional moves (the Humphrey-Roth and Wolpe amendments to legislation to extend the Export Administration Act of 1979) to legislate a full-scope safeguards condition for exports of certain nuclear facility components, heavy water, and nonsensitive nuclear technology that heretofore were handled under procedures distinct from major nuclear exports. Although these proposed legislative changes have not been made final, the retroactive intent of the Wolpe amendment has made completion of the heavy water transfer uncertain.

In the meantime, two important developments in Argentina could affect the nonproliferation outlook in contrasting ways. First, following elections in the fall of 1983, Argentina began a transition from military rule to an elected government led by Raúl Alfonsin and the Radical Civic Union party. Alfonsin made it clear that he expects to reorganize the atomic energy establishment to make it directly accountable to overall government policy, and to ensure that its activities are strictly confined to peaceful purposes. Second, the long-standing head of the nuclear program, Admiral Castro-Madero, disclosed in November 1983 that Argentina had completed the first stage of a uranium enrichment facility begun secretly in 1978 near Pilcaniyeu in Rio Negro province.

This startling disclosure just shortly before Alfonsin's inauguration not only caught the international community off guard but disconcerted the incoming Argentine government. The potential significance for proliferation of an Argentine uranium enrichment capability was lost on no one. The immediate domestic political effect of so dramatically publicizing what the atomic energy management had accomplished to enhance Argentine technological independence, however, was to inject caution into Alfonsin's plans for reorganizing or curtailing the nuclear program. The recent evolution under Alfonsin of Argentina's policy on Tlatelolco ratification and full–scope safeguards shows, as a result, more continuity with traditional policy, and therefore less flexibility, than some had expected.

With the Pilcaniyeu facility, Argentina joins South Africa and Pakistan as developing countries with enrichment programs. Argentina's operational success, incidentally, may predate Pakistan's. And, Argentina is the first country outside the circle of nuclear–weapon powers to rely on gaseous diffusion technology. Technical information about the Argentine enrichment capability is exceedingly sketchy but suggests that the immediate plant is designed not for weapons-grade material but rather for low levels of enrichment. To modify it for weapons-grade material is theoretically possible, but the more plausible danger from a proliferation standpoint would be Argentina's using the technical experience thus acquired to build an additional plant specifically designed for high enrichment levels. By admitting Hans Blix, director-general of the IAEA, to tour the facility, Argentina provided some reassurance about its peaceful purposes, but the Pilcaniyeu disclosure clearly testifies to the great importance of persuading Argentina to adopt full–scope safeguards. Current Argentine policy seems to be one disposed to negotiate on this issue within a Tlatelolco but not an NPT framework.

One other implication of the Argentine enrichment plant deserves mention. Argentina is one of the emerging second-tier nuclear suppliers, as evidenced by the sale several years ago of a research reactor to Peru and similar offers to other countries in South America. The enrichment plant apparently would enable Argentina to supply directly the limited quantities of 20 percent-enriched uranium needed for the Peruvian and other promised research reactors and to enhance its own nuclear export program. Castro-Madero's announcement referred to this aspect of Argentina's new capability as one of "geopolitical" significance, hinting that policies of technological denial ultimately have the effect of increasing the technical independence of developing nations who come to believe they must master the technologies on their own. The effects of the post-Falklands political change in Argentina on the nuclear program, however, not only improved the climate for nonproliferation progress in this particular case (and did force disclosure) but served as a reminder that even nonproliferation policies that merely buy time may in some cases be critical in their own way.

The Mexican case posed a challenge to U.S. nuclear export controls on sensitive nuclear technology, controls that predate the NNPA. Mexico, both an NPT and a Tlatelolco party, has excellent nonproliferation credentials and is also a newcomer to nuclear energy. Hence, it is not a problem country in the traditional sense. Once Mexico made it clear that it expected to put part of its proceeds from oil and natural gas into nuclear power, however, it became a market of great interest to North American and European nuclear vendors. With the arrival of the Reagan administration, Mexico invited bids on planned power reactors and asked suppliers to discuss as a discretionary matter what they would be prepared to offer by way of assistance with sensitive reprocessing and enrichment technology. Because Mexico is an NPT party, full-scope safeguards were not an issue: the question was whether the members of the Nuclear Suppliers Group would countenance the supply of sensitive nuclear technology to a less-developed country having a nascent nuclear power program.

The Reagan commitment to promote nuclear energy and to expand exports, together with the United States' traditionally preferential treatment of Mexico as an important, friendly neighbor, meant that the Mexican request presented an exceptionally acute challenge. The whole business was reminiscent of the problem of ''sweeteners,'' which had engendered the 1975 controversy over the West German contract to sell Brazil sensitive technology as part of a large power reactor package. Very much aware that the attitudes of several other members of the Nuclear Suppliers Group are more permissive, U.S. nuclear vendors were anxious to avoid losing any competitive edge because of a more restrictive U.S. export policy. As it turned out, the U.S. response to Mexico was ambiguous—indicating neither a clear willingness to sell sensitive technology nor intent to deny it. In essence, the United States proposed discussion of a range of ideas in terms of their economic and technological feasibility for Mexico. However, Mexican interest became dormant when financial difficulties forced cancellation of nuclear power projects about three years ago. Thus, the Mexican test was not fully felt. A future revival of Mexican nuclear development plans, however, could revive this challenge to U.S. policies of restraint in supplying sensitive nuclear technology.

South Africa may be considered a quasi-nuclear power. It has developed an indigenous uranium-enrichment capability and, in 1977, seemed to be preparing for a nuclear test in the Kalahari (until reconnaissance satellites detected the installation and the superpowers brought counterpressure into play). Moreover, a peculiar light flash detected by satellite sensors over the South Atlantic in the autumn of 1979 had a signature like that of a nuclear explosion, and suspicions that this may have been a South African nuclear test have not been fully laid to rest.

The Carter policy of gradually escalating pressure on South Africa was modified somewhat by the Reagan administration in order to cultivate constructive engagement. In the field of nuclear cooperation, this has resulted in the loosening of what had become a total embargo on nonsensitive, nuclear-related exports (e.g., equipment for reactor safety or public health) that do not require an NRC export license. As mentioned, the Humphrey-Roth and Wolpe amendments reflect congressional interest in tightening export controls on nuclear components and technologies for which full-scope safeguards are not required and on such Commerce Department–licensed nuclear-usable exports as computers and other dual-use equipment, but new statutory criteria have not yet been established.

Under the Reagan administration, residual U.S. leverage on South Africa through nuclear cooperation has almost completely vanished because of developments in Europe. U.S. leverage derived from an agreement with South Africa that the fuel for the Koeburg power plant, which is being constructed by France, would be supplied by the United States. Under the NNPA, however, the United States could not supply that fuel unless South Africa accepted full-scope safeguards, and this as well as NPT adherence remains Washington's near-term nonproliferation objective in that country. Separately, the United States secured a French commitment not to supply low-enriched uranium fuel for Koeburg. This was important, for other possible suppliers, of which there are very few, were not disposed to sell to South Africa. France nonetheless undercut the arrangement—not by supplying or enriching fuel of its own for South Africa, but by agreeing *to fabricate fuel* delivered to French facilities. South Africa had managed to purchase fuel from an electric-power utility elsewhere in Europe, and that sale was somehow feasible without a government export license because, as far as the utility was concerned, the fuel was being delivered to France for fabrication, not being sent abroad. U.S. firms were apparently involved in brokering the deal. France rationalized its action as merely the fulfillment of a fuel-fabrication service contract, arguing that the agreement was not a contravention of other undertakings. But the fact remains that South Africa and France, perhaps in conjunction with two U.S. firms, circumvented U.S. supply leverage on South Africa by enabling the Koeburg power plant to be fueled for its initial operation.

On the other hand, Reagan administration willingness to authorize U.S. firms to supply technical services for the start–up of the Koeburg power plant, along with other manifestations of "constructive engagement," may have created a climate that facilitated the recent steps of the South African government toward compliance with certain nonproliferation conditions. South Africa announced on 31 January 1984 that it would conduct and administer its nuclear affairs in a manner which is in line with the spirit, principles and goals of the NPT and the Nuclear Suppliers Group guidelines; require safeguards as a condition for exporting nuclear material, equipment, and technology; and require recipients of such exports not only to accept safeguards but also to guarantee not to use the exported items for nuclear explosive purposes. At the same time, South Africa declared its willingness to resume discussions with the IAEA preparatory to placing safeguards on a semicommercial enrichment plant that is still under construction and to resume related discussions with the United States. While these actions were decoupled from U.S. willingness to suspend DOE enrichment contracts and related penalties (similar to the Brazil case), the U.S. movement to resolve these contractual issues was almost simultaneous. The significance was noted officially by the United States, which stated that South Africa's measures "are consistent with efforts by the United

States and other governments to develop a common nuclear supply policy in the interests of limiting the spread of nuclear weapons.''

Israel has posed two special problems for the Reagan administration. The first was Israel's June 1981 air strike on the Osirak (Tammuz I) research reactor near Baghdad. The second, which may partly derive from the Israeli action, was the challenge to Israel's credentials in the 1982 IAEA General Conference. Both developments have profound implications for the future of nonproliferation policy and the efficacy of the IAEA.

The bombing of Osirak (ostensibly a peaceful nuclear facility under IAEA safeguards) represented a serious challenge to the credibility of the IAEA safeguards system and to the fabric of international nuclear cooperation that depends on those safeguards. The Reagan administration therefore condemned the Israeli strike, but was unable to do more. Israel argued that other evidence pointed conclusively to a weapons-development role for Osirak and that, since other measures to prevent operation of the reactor had failed, Israel had no choice but to use force in its self-defense. By striking the reactor before it went critical, the Israelis pointed out, they had eliminated the risk of radiation dispersal.

In the autumn of 1982, a narrow ''majority'' of the IAEA General Conference membership (that majority having been contrived by an erroneous technical ruling) forced a rejection of Israeli credentials as well as Israel's ouster from the conference in its closing hours. Politically, this action was primarily motivated by the events in Lebanon (the massacre at Sabra and Shatila occurred the weekend before the conference convened) but also derived from anger at Israel's bombardment of a peaceful nuclear facility, distress at Israel's intransigence in resisting IAEA safeguards on its own nuclear facilities, general Arab or Muslim state opposition to Israel, and disenchantment with the preferential treatment Israel has received from the West despite its questionable nonproliferation credentials.

But the challenge to Israel's status in the IAEA was also part of a broader attack on Israeli membership in various international organizations, an effort aimed at ostracizing Israel and forcing changes in its policies. The United States traditionally has resisted this politics of exclusion in international organizations because it subverts their fundamental purposes. The Reagan administration had already adopted a tougher stance against challenges to Israeli credentials in the UN General Assembly, and when the challenge was mounted in the IAEA, Washington's response was to withdraw temporarily from participation and to withhold the next installment on U.S. contributions to the agency's budget. Early in 1983, the United States decided to lift its boycott and renew its participation in the agency. Congressional acquiescence in this decision was complicated by an amendment to the continuing appropriations bill in the Ninety-seventh Congress but was made possible by IAEA

Director-General Blix's official statement that Israel is a fully participating member of the agency.

Renewed confrontation over this issue was averted by a compromise in October 1983 at the twenty-seventh session of the IAEA General Conference in which an Iraq-sponsored resolution was adopted in exchange for an understanding that Israel's credentials would not be challenged. The adopted resolution essentially called on Israel "to withdraw forthwith its threat to attack and destroy nuclear facilities in Iraq and other countries" and to redress the destruction Iraq had suffered in 1981, and asked the director-general to report at the next session on the consequences of armed attacks or threatened attacks on peaceful nuclear facilities on the IAEA safeguards system. It remains true, however, that the politics of exclusion might someday lock the United States into a position that threatens the existence of the agency and, ultimately, the international system of nuclear cooperation.

The Pakistan Test Case

Pakistani interest in a nuclear weapons capability was spurred by India's nuclear test in 1974. In 1979, about a year after France had canceled a contract to supply a reprocessing facility, it became known that Pakistan had embarked on a covert uranium-enrichment program, secretly procuring gas-centrifuge design information from the URENCO consortium and components from European suppliers. Apparently, Pakistan also continued a small-scale, unsafeguarded reprocessing project after France withdrew its cooperation. These disclosures forced the Carter administration to invoke the sanctions of the Symington and Glenn amendments to the Foreign Assistance Act, cutting off all military and most economic assistance to Pakistan in the spring of 1979.

In December of the same year, the Soviet Union invaded Afghanistan, creating a direct threat to Pakistan's security. With Iran in the throes of revolutionary turmoil, the Soviet move also posed a new strategic threat to the security of the Persian Gulf states and to the West's supply of oil from that region. In January 1980, the Carter Doctrine, which declared a vital U.S. interest in the region and a commitment to repel external military aggression, was proclaimed. Carter also offered to restore U.S. military and economic assistance to Pakistan with a two-year, $400 million package—which Pakistan's President Zia scornfully described as "peanuts."

The Carter offer responded to the new strategic situation, not to any nonproliferation assurances from Pakistan. Since Pakistan continued its unsafeguarded development of sensitive nuclear technology, the renewal of assistance could not be implemented without repeal or modification of the Symington and Glenn amendments, or a presidential waiver subject to congressional approval. The history of strained U.S. relations with Pakistan remained an obstacle until after the Reagan administration took office.

President Reagan adopted an even more affirmative stand on security and economic assistance to Pakistan, pledging a six-year package with a $3.2 billion price tag and including a commitment to sell forty F-16 fighter aircraft. This was seen as a far more serious proposal than anything offered by the Carter administration. The offer of the F-16—one of the most sophisticated and capable fighter-interceptors in the world today and a mainstay of the U.S. Air Force for tactical missions—symbolized a strong commitment to Pakistani security and put the administration's prestige on the line in dealing with the U.S. Congress. Pakistan welcomed this show of support and did its part to put the relationship on a firmer basis. Subsequently, Reagan won congressional support for a one-time exemption to the Symington and Glenn amendments, thus permitting implementation of the assistance offered to Pakistan.

The Reagan policy toward Pakistan is a test of the political approach to nonproliferation. It is based on the premise that the generous supply of conventional military equipment heightens the recipient's sense of security and by the same token diminishes the incentives for nuclear weapons acquisition. Rather than enforce undiluted sanctions, which may only strengthen local determination to develop an independent nuclear capability, the Reagan philosophy is to buy out the temptation to proliferate. The approach is not necessarily devoid of sanctions; instead, it expands the scope of potential sanctions, but holds them in abeyance as a deterrent. This is done as a complement to, rather than a substitute for, continued consultation with suppliers to prevent Pakistani procurement of sensitive nuclear technology or related components.

Recent developments in the People's Republic of China (PRC) have reduced the concern that Chinese nuclear exports or assistance might contribute to nuclear proliferation in Pakistan (or other developing countries). Despite an early posture that could have been interpreted to welcome proliferation in the Third World, China has moved within the last year to adopt a much more reassuring position. The PRC joined the IAEA formally on New Year's Day 1984. Later the same month, the Chinese prime minister declared in the White House: "We do not engage in nuclear proliferation ourselves, nor do we help other countries develop nuclear weapons." Clarifications were later offered that the oral pledge applies to the future and encompasses nuclear explosives as well as nuclear weapons. These indications and China's willingness to meet U.S. export conditions (including consent rights on the subsequent disposition or retransfer of U.S. nuclear technology, material, or material used in U.S.-origin facilities) paved the way for the signing of a United States-China peaceful nuclear cooperation agreement in April 1984.

Independent technical development of sensitive nuclear technology in Pakistan, however, remains a matter of concern. President Zia ul-Haq has provided assurances that all of Pakistan's nuclear activities are peaceful, but recorded statements of the late Pakistani prime minister reflect the popular assumption today in Pakistan and its press that the nuclear program is in fact intended to provide a weapons capability. And suggestive discussions by former Pakistani officials—as well as a February 1984 press interview in which Pakistani enrichment program leader Abdul Qadir Khan stated that certain technical barriers had been overcome—provide good cause for congressional and administration concern. Although a nuclear explosive test by Pakistan could easily provoke a full-fledged Indian nuclear weapons program, the same result might occur if India detected undeclared and still untested nuclear explosive devices. If deterrent sanctions are to be effective against proliferation in Pakistan, responsive policy mechanisms need to be devised that are able to define and detect thresholds in a concealed process that avoids resort to direct nuclear explosive testing by taking covert proliferation steps, such as stockpiling nuclear weapons material or components, or developing something resembling a "bomb in the basement" or a so-called peaceful nuclear explosive capability.

It remains to be seen whether the administration's nonproliferation strategy stressing security incentives will work in Pakistan. It does seem unlikely that Pakistan would jeopardize the new U.S. aid pipeline by overtly demonstrating a nuclear-explosive capability merely because such a technical threshold has been reached. But it is clear that Pakistan could also lie low until the six-year package has been fully delivered. There is also some danger that this approach makes the United States susceptible to a form of blackmail by proliferators. Since no one seems able to devise a better plan for the Pakistani situation and India seems disinclined even to try, the Reagan administration's effort deserves maximum support.

There is also a remote chance that Pakistan, as it gains confidence in improved conventional security arrangements, will decide to put aside the nuclear weapons option. Economic planners in Pakistan have revived interest in the potential for nuclear energy in Pakistan's industrial development. Pakistan is now soliciting foreign supplier bids for the construction of a 900-megawatt power plant at Chasma and is actively seeking World Bank and other loan assistance for its energy programs. The NNPA, unless it is amended, would prohibit U.S. vendors or construction firms from direct participation, and the U.S. strongly urged other suppliers to withhold participation unless Pakistan indicates a willingness to accept full-scope safeguards. It is not unreasonable to explore the possibility that Pakistan might be reintegrated into the system of peaceful international nuclear cooperation in exchange for accepting full-scope safeguards and providing appropriate proof that the weapons option has been dropped.

The Reagan approach to the problem countries overall shows more continuity than major shifts in nonproliferation policy. This is as it should be, for the fundamental objectives and legal arrangements of nonproliferation remain the same. The shifts are in attitude and in the orchestration of a wider array of policy instruments. Greater emphasis is being placed on positive nonproliferation incentives. Sanctions and punitive elements of nonproliferation policy have not been discarded, but they have been brought into what is arguably a more realistic balance with positive assistance. Moreover, sanctions tend to be handled through quiet diplomacy rather than by methods that are more likely to escalate into public confrontation.

The Reagan approach to the problem countries is also better adjusted to the requirements of industrialized countries (especially those in the Organization for Economic Cooperation and Development) whose nuclear energy commitments are very substantial and regarded as crucial to energy security. Supplier coordination is much more likely to be achieved if the United States plays an affirmative rather than a skeptical role in nuclear energy development in advanced industrial settings. There are appropriate grounds in time and place for different approaches to nuclear energy—some suitable for advanced industrial countries, others for those at a much less advanced stage of industrial development. In this regard, it is high time that international acceptance of appropriate criteria be promoted in the relevant consultative and institutional bodies.

There will always be some anguish in fitting general legislative requirements to specific cases. The need for executive branch flexibility in administering legal guidelines will remain. Whatever the outcome of test cases, such as that posed by Pakistan today, the need to prevent additional proliferation will remain. Policy innovation will continue to digest the lessons of experience. In the ebb and flow of partisan electoral politics, there is always some danger that a few individuals, isolationist in predisposition or otherwise unacquainted with the way the world works, will rise to positions of power and temporarily derail important aspects of U.S. foreign policy. Fortunately, that danger does not seem to loom large in the nonproliferation policy area today. But if it did, other advanced nuclear countries and the problem countries—in quite different ways—would prod us to get policy back on track.

9

Is Further Proliferation of Nuclear Weapons Irrelevant to U.S. National Security?

Robert E. Pendley

For almost four decades, the United States has insisted that any increase in the number of states possessing nuclear weapons should be discouraged, claiming that nuclear proliferation would undermine international security and stability, and threaten the national security interests of the United States. From the abortive Baruch Plan proposed by the Truman administration, to the enunciation of Reagan administration policy on nuclear cooperation and non-proliferation, U.S. law and policy have consistently articulated the belief that the possibility of nuclear weapons proliferation is real, and that its occurrence endangers the interests of the United States. This view was clearly emphasized by the Reagan administration when the president on 16 July 1981 stated that the basis of U.S. nonproliferation policy was to "establish the prevention of the spread of nuclear weapons as a fundamental national security and foreign policy objective."[1]

We continue to declare the significance of nonproliferation policy for U.S. national security. But do we really mean it any longer? Has the historical experience of the last four decades supported or undermined our confidence in the proposition that further nuclear weapons proliferation is counter to the interests of the United States? Should we go on believing in its undesirability, and persevere in the always difficult, and sometimes frustrating and embarrassing political and diplomatic efforts required to curb the spread of the bomb?

Contrary to the original perception that further weapons proliferation was imminent and certainly harmful to U.S. interests, a view has emerged that holds the original perception to be wrongheaded. It asserts that proliferation not only has not been harmful but may have been beneficial. From this

---

The opinions expressed in this article are those of the author and are not intended to represent those of his employer.

perspective, the nonproliferation policies that the United States has laboriously implemented through the years in service to the perception of danger are at best irrelevant to our own national security. At worst, they can be injurious to our more important international interests.

The new view seems to be based on three agruments. The first questions the facts of the case by noting that despite the alarms raised early in the nuclear era about the impending danger of the proliferation of nuclear weapons capabilities to large numbers of states, the total number of states that have actually decided to detonate nuclear explosive devices or build nuclear weapons arsenals has been very small. Appealing to the inertia of history, this view argues further that the future will resemble the past, and that we should not expect to see rapid or extensive proliferation of weapons states in the future.

The second argument challenges the logic of the case, questioning the very premise of nonproliferation efforts by asserting that the alleged dangers of proliferation have been presumed rather than demonstrated. This view argues that the actual political effects of the limited spread of nuclear capabilities, as it has occurred historically, have been good rather than bad for global and regional stability, and have actually served to reduce levels of international conflict.

The third argument draws upon and extends the previous two. It assumes that future proliferation is probably not a direct threat to the security of the United States, even if it should occur, and concludes that concerns within the United States for implementing nonproliferation measures involve wasted effort.

How much credence should we give these arguments? Do they undermine the premise of the traditional policy position of the United States, which holds that any further proliferation of nuclear weapons is bad, and is to be prohibited if possible? Is it time to abandon our nonproliferation policies of almost forty years?

No Apocalypse Now

To be sure, the early analytical literature on the prospects for nuclear proliferation, and its effects on world stability were near-apocalyptic in character. Forecasts of ten, twenty, or even more nuclear powers emerging by the 1970s were common in early writings. There seemed to be general agreement that if more than, say, five major world powers possessed these weapons, it would be inevitable that they would be used in a major nuclear conflict. Megadeaths and destruction of unimaginable proportions would result. Reality has not been nearly so dramatic. Only six nuclear-weapon states exist, and only five of these have assembled significant arsenals of deliverable nuclear explosives. No military use of nuclear weapons has occurred since 1945, and the frictions between nuclear-weapon states have not resulted in major armed conflict between them, especially not a nuclear conflict. Also, almost none of the potentially numerous states with a clear capability or reasonable opportunity to develop nuclear weapons technologies has apparently chosen to do so. It seems as if one should conclude that most states have found nuclear weapons would not serve their national interests. Why should this not continue to be the case in the future? And, because further proliferation is unlikely to occur, why should we worry?

But there are in effect two kinds of nuclear powers: those who have "weaponized" (i.e. who have engineered and stockpiled sufficient nuclear devices to cause large-scale damage in a conflict), and those who have become "weapons-capable" (i.e. who have accumulated enough nuclear scientific information, and perhaps enough access to technologies and nuclear materials to be able to launch a nuclear weapons construction program if they wish to do so).

Focusing attention on the fact that only five national governments have chosen to become weaponized nuclear powers obscures an equally compelling fact: the proliferation of weapons-capable states has already occurred on a large scale. Numerous governments in all regions of the world have built up the knowledge base and the critical mass of trained people sufficient to construct nuclear weapons, should they decide to do so. Further, this has been accompanied by an unparalleled, drastic increase in the worldwide availability of nuclear equipment, materials, and technologies that either are now already capable of being, or could readily be, converted to military uses.

But one reason we have little to fear from proliferation, the argument goes, is the undeniable fact that the great majority of states now believe that the acquisition of nuclear weapons would not improve their security, and could, in certain circumstances, diminish it. While this argument has merit, it ignores the fact that the security interests and perceptions that have led countries such as Canada, Sweden, Japan, and the Federal Republic of Germany to forgo nuclear weapons could change over time. If U.S. nuclear guarantees lose their credibility, if there is a dramatic downturn in East-West relations, or if other drastic upheavals in the existing international security system should occur, the nuclear option may be reconsidered by certain non-nuclear-weapon states. Furthermore, this argument does not sufficiently account for the development of nuclear weapons capabilities or options in Nonproliferation Treaty (NPT) holdout states such as Israel, South Africa, India, and Pakistan or the nuclear weapon ambitions of NPT parties like Libya. And, it disregards the domino effect that has been noted with respect to past proliferation.

Another, far less compelling, reason for minimizing the proliferation danger assumes the efficacy of the international nonproliferation regime, complete with international organizations and developing international moral and legal norms that militate against the very legitimacy of acquiring nuclear weapons, that was slowly constructed during the past thirty years. This regime, relying largely upon the "no-weapons" pledges undertaken in the NPT and the Treaty of Tlatelolco, and depending on the ability of the International Atomic Energy Agency and its safeguards systems to assure the peaceful intent and use of nuclear facilities and materials, assures us that the spread of nuclear technologies and materials will not lead to the future spread of further weaponry. Or, so we are supposed to believe.

But this analysis assumes a linear progression toward more and more support for the nonproliferation regime. It ignores the fact that the central legal element of the regime, the NPT, was viewed by many signatory states as having force for only a limited period. During this time, the existing weaponized nuclear powers—especially the United States and the Soviet Union—undertook to experiment with nuclear arms control and disarmament. The non-nuclear-weapon states expected that while the NPT is in force, significant reductions in nuclear arsenals would be agreed to, limitations or bans on nuclear explosive testing would be established, and some progress toward nuclear disarmament would be made.

These expectations have not been met, and the United States and the Soviet Union are seen by many states as less than serious about their arms control commitments under the treaty. Support for continuing the nonproliferation regime has become uncertain in some governments, and others have been increasingly unwilling to take further steps to strengthen and broaden the coverage of the regime. Some highly placed international figures have speculated that unless the United States and the Soviet Union reach some meaningful and binding nuclear arms control agreement soon, the foundation of the nonproliferation regime will begin to crack as several parties to it renounce their commitment to abstain from nuclear weapons, or depart the NPT regime.[2]

So it is not so clear that the current "nonproliferation" situation is such a good one, or that proliferation has been successfully contained. The number of weapons-capable states has clearly grown. And the means of becoming a weaponized nuclear power are increasingly, and increasingly easily, available. Can we assume that current security interests and policies, which have led many states to forgo nuclear weapons, will persist indefinitely? Can we rely upon an international monitoring regime for encouraging and helping to verify nonproliferation goals that has been threatened by the intrusion of extraneous political factors, and may be directly challenged in the future? What are the consequences of proliferation in any one of several regions of the world where the United States has explicit national security interests at stake?

Are More Better?

Perhaps we should not worry, for perhaps more nuclear weapons would be better, rather than worse, for world and regional stability. This argument has been made by some who challenge the conventional wisdom that the increasing nuclear weapons capability in the world implies an increased risk of nuclear war and decreased security for the United States.[3]

According to this line of argument, after the early days of the nuclear era, during which the use of nuclear weapons was contemplated for military operational purposes, the strategy supporting nuclear arsenals very rapidly evolved to the concept of deterrence through the threat of unacceptable nuclear retaliation against nuclear attack. On the basis of the behavior of the weaponized nuclear powers during and after the period in which they constructed their nuclear forces, and the fact that since 1945 these forces have not been employed in the service of any military objective other than to stalemate other nuclear powers, the conclusion is drawn that nuclear weapons are now constructed and deployed so as to have only the purpose of deterring adversaries, particularly adversaries with nuclear weapons of their own.

Those who argue this way observe that in the past proliferation has not significantly altered international relations, regional power balances, or alliance structures. Neither has it led to increased conflict. In fact, it appears that in some cases nuclear powers became more cautious and circumspect in their political behavior, leading to increased rather than lessened stability in their relationships with others.[4]

Further, the argument goes, creation of small nuclear forces by new nuclear powers may similarly stabilize relationships between hostile regional powers and reduce the probability of overt conflict among them. The very nature of nuclear weapons, which are capable of causing immense damage with relatively few, small weapons, means that nuclear forces meant for deterrence by threat of unacceptable punishment are absolute, not relative. Therefore a small nuclear force, offering the threat of second-strike punitive nuclear attacks, is all that is required. The nuclear deterrent force can be modest in number, and may be relatively insensitive to the magnitude and dimensions of potential military threats posed by opponents. Because the only reason for constructing a nuclear arsenal would be to secure the deterrence desired, and not to provide for a "war-fighting" defense, neither regional nor global stability would be upset by new threats of nuclear-armed adventurism. All sides know this, so the deterrent force accomplishes its mission the instant it is formed.

To the challenge of critics who claim that the concept of punitive, mutual deterrence, and the ability to implement and sustain such a system may be unique to the existing nuclear-weapon states, the advocates of this school of thought respond with charges of ethnocentrism. What right or reason do we have to presume that others are less reasonable than we when it comes to securing the interests of their nation? Why should we assume that others would act less rationally with respect to using nuclear weapons? Because the weapons are so obviously dangerous and damaging, all states that have so far possessed them have emphasized their deterrent role, and have not employed them for any military "war–fighting" purpose. Is it not reasonable to suppose, and project, that new possessors of the weapons will behave similarly, and acquire the capability only for their own deterrent needs?

This reasoning offers a distorted picture of actual deterrent relationships and nuclear strategies among existing nuclear-weapon states. And, it confuses the relationship between the deterrent function of nuclear weapons and their ability to be used in a conflict. Moreover, the argumentation embodies an ethnocentric error of its own: the presumptuous projection of our own values, calculations of rationality, and politico-strategic situation onto other nations. The argument seeks to become a self-fulfilling prophecy, to reassure us that there is no danger from further proliferation of weaponized states. It simply assumes, in a putative fashion, that new nuclear-weapon states will behave in the future as we have in the past.

But this ignores the fact that nuclear weapons have been used in the past, and could be used again. Some states (even the major nuclear powers) may seek to acquire them precisely to use them in certain critical situations; without realistic plans to do so, even a punitive deterrent strategy would be useless. Consider the obvious example of one nuclear-capable state, Israel. It exists in a region of surrounding hostile powers, with little hope of forming long-lasting regional security arrangements based upon common political, cultural, or ethnic values. Its geostrategic situation involves threats to its very existence as a nation, and to its people as well. The strategic situations we face, and our choices about the possible uses of nuclear weapons to deal with them, are truly different from and incomparable to those of Israel. The feasibility or durability of a punitive, mutual deterrence policy in the Middle East must at least be open to grave doubts.

Why should we assume that new nuclear powers who might assemble only relatively small nuclear arsenals would do so only for punitive deterrent purposes? Might not governments of other countries, perceiving their people, culture, and heritage at stake, react differently and more severely? In light of the growing conventional capabilities of its regional adversaries, and the increasing costs of a credible conventional defense, we can imagine Israel's future reliance on tactical nuclear weapons to defeat a conventional attack. There are those in Israel who have spoken of nuclear exchanges between Israel and its enemies. More recently, commenting on the use of chemical weapons in the Iran-Iraq war, a Likud member of the Israeli Knesset observed that it had happened before in the region despite the nominal adherance of the combatants to the Geneva Convention. He noted that the Arab states signatory to that convention are also parties to the NPT. If they are willing to violate one arms control treaty, he questioned rhetorically, why should they be expected to observe the other? He was led to "the realization that nonconventional warfare may become an immediate possibility, and that Israel will have to prepare for it."[5]

As the Israeli case illustrates, new nuclear powers might not be wedded to punitive, mutual deterrence concepts, as the advocates of this school would suggest. Even if we should convince ourselves that further use of nuclear weapons is inconceivable for our own purposes, we must not rule out the real possibility that others face very different national security conditions. They may find the perceived military utility of nuclear weapons precisely the reason for having them. More nuclear powers may be worse for the regions that experience them.

Implications for United States Security

But even if these fears are justified, and the original speculations about the possibilities for nuclear conflict as a result of further weapons proliferation were correct, what does this mean for U.S. security and military contingency thinking? Some believe that even if a worst case were to occur, with actual military use of one or more nuclear explosions outside the territory of the existing nuclear powers, the security of the United States would not be affected. It is difficult to counter this. Underlying the assertion seems to be the assumption that the United States can isolate itself from the political and military actions that new possessors of nuclear weapons may take, no matter how radical. The notion of an antiseptic atomic attack by others against others, neatly contained in a distant part of the world, which does not involve U.S. territory and personnel and is surgically separated from any real geopolitical or security interests of the United States, seems to characterize this viewpoint. The shakiness of this assumption can be assessed by consulting several counterexamples that examine the specific links between the United States and some of the "problem countries" more likely than others to be involved in conflicts with nuclear dimensions in the future, the motivations that might stimulate use of nuclear explosions, and how they could affect the United States.

The United States has direct stakes in the continued political stability and survival of nations in the Middle East and South America because of the direct threats to its economic, political, and alliance interests should these regions become unstable or should vital threats be made against states in the region. In the Middle East, we usually focus on our relations with Israel and our continued concern for its security, and it is difficult to conceive that the international position of the United States would be unaltered if a nuclear attack on Israel destroyed the country. However, Israel may be the party that has to initiate a nuclear confrontation if faced with a threat to its national survival. This could bring about threats to another key security interest of the United States. We need only think of our interest in assuring the continued flow of crude oil from the region to our European and Japanese allies, and to ourselves. In the past, Islamic states have reacted to serious conflicts with Israel by attempting reprisals against the West, including oil embargoes. It is inconceivable that a nuclear strike undertaken by, or against, Israel would not put our interests at risk once again.

Similarly in South America, it is inconceivable that the threat or actual use of nuclear weapons by either Argentina or Brazil would not have serious political fallout. Any subsequent attempts by the United States to maintain amicable economic and political relationships with these Latin American states would be adversely affected. In addition, we surely cannot discount or ignore the effects on the international and the U.S. banking and financial systems should such major regional powers, with massive indebtedness to the West, collapse in a nuclear abyss.

Another possibility is that the United States could not remain wholly removed from some nuclear conflicts, and would itself be almost inevitably drawn into them through explicit security links and long-standing political commitments to provide security assurances to other states. For example, situations involving attacks on, or by, a nuclear-armed South Korea probably could not be ignored by the United States, given U.S. military deployments in the area and the security guarantees we have granted to the South Koreans for decades. Similar commitments have been made to Israel, and there would be pressure within the United States to become seriously involved if the government of Taiwan encountered a grave threat with a nuclear dimension. In all of these instances, reasons would probably be compelling for intervention by the United States in some form, with relations with both our security partners and others in the area drastically changed.

The United States could be involved indirectly in cases that in themselves do not present compelling evidence for its direct action. The potential for the escalation through a nuclear threshold of hostilities between South Africa and its black African neighbor states is real. Should the South African regime feel forced to meet a perceived invasion force, or other vital threat, with a nuclear response, the states of the region could resist with revulsion toward the United States and its policies in the area. Even if the United States attempted to remain above the fray in these instances the possibilities for long-term damage to political relationships with other major regional powers is clear and evident.

The United States itself might become a target in a nuclear conflict that appears to involve only others. The question of nuclear terrorism against the United States has been debated frequently, with a major conclusion that the country is effectively open to assault. Would-be assailants lack only the motivation and material to mount a nuclear attack and, perhaps, the desire to suffer the expected consequences. The involvement of their country in a nuclear engagement with a power seen as friendly to, supported by, or acting as a surrogate for the United States could provide motivation sufficient for them to take the chance. These possibilities could take the form of small groups acting alone, but consistently, in their view, with their nation's interest. It might even take the form of state terrorism. The increasingly advanced weapons-delivery-system capabilities of some nations in problem areas, together with possession of or access to nuclear explosives, could constitute a potent threat to the security of the land mass and population centers of the United States itself.

Finally, we should consider the degree of vulnerability of U.S. military assets deployed in regions of political hostility and military volatility. The United States itself has over the years contemplated the battlefield use of nuclear weapons as a means of overcoming substantial military odds. Why should the same idea not occur to others who find themselves in a conflict and are faced with impending defeat? Forces of the United States that may be identified with antagonists, or that may simply be targets of opportunity, may become vulnerable to potential nuclear attacks.

Military Contingencies and Considerations

The purpose of raising these speculations is not to make predictions. Rather, it is intended to counter the argument that further nuclear weapons proliferation is irrelevant to the national security interests of the United States. The United States will very likely find itself at least very much affected and possibly involved if proliferation occurs in certain regions or under certain circumstances. This conclusion implies that we should begin to engage in serious military analysis and planning for the possibility that these kinds of situations may occur so as to be able to prevent or to dominate the course of nuclear events that impact seriously on our interests. Several different kinds of military considerations arise from the previous thoughts.

One immediate conclusion is that the potential role and military makeup of a U.S. rapid deployment force (RDF) may have to be redefined. Planners may have to consider the possible requirement for RDF deployment and commitment in nuclear confrontations as well as conventional engagements, and in locations that may not be amendable to preplanning. The RDF mission in such situations may be to field a force capable of intervening to deter or to stop the escalation of a nuclear confrontation in areas as widely separated as South America, Southwest Asia, the Middle East, or Africa. As well, there is the possible need to carry out assignments in an operational environment in which the use of nuclear weapons is threatened or has occurred. The capabilities and special training required of such an RDF go well beyond current plans.

The means of committing U.S. forces abroad may also require close attention. The Falklands campaign pointed out not only the difficulty in bringing force to bear at a great distance but also the vulnerability of distant forces and of the supply lines needed to keep them operational. Carrying out a similar operation against a nuclear-armed opponent, even one with a tiny nuclear arsenal, will add to the complexity and uncertainty of such missions.

There is also the question of how such forces are to be armed if they are to deal with nuclear crises. Current public accounts of the RDF do not envision its commitment in nuclear situations, and nuclear weapons do not appear to be within its intended capabilities. Should we reconsider the role of U.S. tactical nuclear forces, and the possibility that mobile, rapidly deployable nuclear capabilities may be required in the future?

The proliferation to some nuclear-capable states of advanced military technologies that can become future delivery means for nuclear attacks against the United States may require explicit attention. Of particular concern are the implications of the developing nuclear-submarine capabilities of nations such as Brazil and Argentina, and the rapidly growing competence in ballistic missile technology of a number of nations, including India and the People's Republic of China. These trends may indicate the need for reconsidering defenses against ballistic missile attacks that may not take the form of strategic nuclear conflict but, rather, of limited, short-range attacks launched from just beyond U.S. borders. Military defensive alternatives for such assignments might more closely resemble classical air and coastal defenses than current strategic ballistic missile defense concepts.

At a different level, the possible long-term impact of further proliferation on the strategic nuclear relationship should be considered as well. Most advanced nuclear-capable states have so far decided against developing nuclear weapons; this includes undertakings by Japan and West Germany not to acquire nuclear capabilities. But if a South Korea or a Taiwan decided to pursue nuclear weaponry, would Japan's commitment to forgo the nuclear option be kept? Would similar events on the periphery of Europe not provoke a West German reaction? And if such events should lead to a change of course on the part of our allies, can we believe that our relationships with them, and with the Soviet Union, will remain the same?

And, finally, the United States, in addition to considering preparation of reactive measures in anticipation of these contingencies, may want to take preemptive or preventive steps now to assure that they do not occur. If the drive to assemble further nuclear weapons arsenals is motivated by concerns, sometimes desperate, about national security and survival, then the United States may need to reconsider appropriate combinations of military assistance and mutual security arrangements and guarantees so as to head off nuclear possibilities. President Reagan himself suggested this course of action in his July 1981 nonproliferation policy statement:

In the final analysis, the success of our efforts depends on our ability to improve regional and global stability and reduce those motivations that can drive countries toward nuclear explosives. This calls for a strong and dependable United States, vibrant alliances and improved relations with others, and a dedication to those tasks that are vital for a stable world order.[6]

The president's national security adviser has recently reemphasized this point, saying that enhancing strategic stability and reducing nuclear weapons stockpiles will not solve our nuclear concerns "if we neglect . . . the spread of nuclear weapons." He asserted that "reducing the conditions that give rise to proliferation must be the central premise of our nonproliferation policy."[7] However, actual implementation of this policy, seeking to obviate moves toward increased regional nuclear capabilities, will call for a variety of bilateral security dealings with so-called problem countries in regions important to the United States, relationships that U.S. governments have been largely chary of so far. It will also require discrimination and forcefulness in identifying the security interests of the United States in these key regions, and crafting specific foreign policies to further those interests.

Notes

1. Ronald Reagan, "Statement on United States Nuclear Nonproliferation and Peaceful Nuclear Cooperation Policy," 16 July 1981.
2. Such an argument was made, for example, by Sigvard Eklund, former director-general of the IAEA, in a speech at a commemorative conference, Atoms for Peace After Thirty Years, 7-8 December 1983, Washington, D.C.
3. The most notable exponent of this theme is Kenneth Waltz. See his *The Spread of Nuclear Weapons: More May Be Better*, Adelphi Paper No. 171 (London: International Institute of Strategic Studies, Autumn 1981).
4. Ibid., pp. 3-7.
5. Joseph T. Rom, "Poison Gas and the Death of Treaties," *Washington Post*, 5 April 1984.
6. Reagan, "Statement." (See note 1 above.)
7. Robert C. McFarlane, "Effective Arms Control, Challenge of the 1980s," address, Center for Law and National Security, Charlottesville, Virginia, 22 June 1984.

10

Arms Control, Nonproliferation, and U.S. National Security

Joseph F. Pilat

In his statement to the UN Special Session on Disarmament in June 1982, Hans Blix, the director-general of the International Atomic Energy Agency (IAEA) recalled that the Treaty on the Nonproliferation of Nuclear Weapons (NPT) envisaged a world without nuclear weapons. He warned that, unless the nuclear-weapon states made serious moves toward controlling nuclear arms and eventual disarmament, further proliferation loomed.[1] Blix may have thought it wise, or perhaps was compelled, to overemphasize the dangers of further proliferation posed by the superpower arms race, but his remarks mirrored the sentiments expressed by the majority of states at the Second NPT Review Conference and suggest that it is becoming increasingly difficult to isolate nonproliferation from nuclear disarmament. Ever since the dawn of the nuclear era, there has been a critical link between nuclear disarmament and nonproliferation; the nature of this critical link is unclear, however, and frequently the link is ignored or denied.

On the one hand, nuclear deterrence based on strong superpower nuclear arsenals is believed to inhibit nuclear proliferation. It has been correctly understood that nuclear deterrence has promoted security and stability, particularly in Europe and the Far East. And, it is recognized that reductions in the nuclear arsenal of the United States, if they undermined the vitality of U.S. deterrence strategy, could reduce the credibility of U.S. nuclear guarantees, creating among U.S. allies a sense of insecurity that could lead them to "go nuclear." On the other hand, it is often argued that the failure of the superpowers to agree to reductions of their nuclear arsenals, and their continued reliance on nuclear deterrence are a major spur to nuclear proliferation. Public

The opinions expressed here are those of the author and are not intended to represent those of his employer.

concern about this linkage between nuclear deterrence and nonproliferation generally derives from fears engendered by what appear to be too many nuclear weapons, and the superpower arms race. The continuation of the arms race and the failure of arms control and disarmament negotiations lend support to the belief that U.S. and Soviet power, prestige, and security depend upon nuclear weapons. Therefore, the argument goes, the non-nuclear-weapon states (particularly those that are not allied with nuclear-weapon states and do not share their nuclear shield) may conclude that they would be well served by possession of these weapons. In this sense, the failure of nuclear arms reductions could create incentives for further proliferation.

Because the relationship between superpower nuclear forces and nonproliferation has these two opposing aspects, it is not surprising that the United States, like the Soviet Union, has traditionally resisted acknowledging the linkage between nonproliferation and nuclear disarmament that other states profess to see. To continue to do so in present circumstances, however, could work to the detriment of U.S. security interests. It could further exacerbate tensions between the nuclear haves and have-nots and erode the international nonproliferation regime, the foundation of which is the NPT and its explicit rights and obligations. And, if ever the U.S. nuclear freeze movement and the European nuclear disarmament movement choose to recognize and popularize this criticial link, a continuation of past U.S. policy could have adverse implications for U.S. domestic politics as well as for U.S. relations with NATO.

Implied Linkages

The Reagan administration's nonproliferation policy never refers explicitly to nuclear arms control and disarmament, nor does it recognize any nuclear disarmament-nonproliferation relationship. Nevertheless, elements of the policy at least imply a linkage between nuclear arms control and nonproliferation. The Reagan administration views nonproliferation as primarily a political problem, directly related to the security interests and perspectives of possible proliferants. Of this, on 16 July 1981, President Reagan said:

> The problem of reducing the risks of nuclear proliferation has many aspects. . . . In the final analysis, the success of our efforts [to deal with it effectively] depends on our ability to improve regional and global stability and reduce those motivations that can drive countries toward nuclear explosives. This calls for a strong and dependable United States, vibrant alliances and improved relations with others, and a dedication to those tasks that are vital for a stable world order.[2]

Administration officials have on other occasions highlighted this premise, which suggests the political advantages of linking nonproliferation initiatives to U.S. security agreements with non-nuclear-weapon states as well as to ongoing arms control negotiations. To date, though, the only significant case in which a U.S. security agreement has been overtly affected by an interest in reducing proliferation pressures on a non-nuclear-weapon state—i.e. Pakistan—involved U.S. economic and military assistance rather than positive or negative nuclear assurances. And, it appears that the administration's arms control policy and proposals have largely been formulated in isolation from nonproliferation policy and objectives. However, in a 31 March 1983 speech on arms control policy, Reagan did tentatively link his "interim proposal" for the Geneva intermediate-range nuclear force (INF) talks to nonproliferation. He noted that for arms control to be truly complete and world security strengthened, "we must also increase our efforts to halt the spread of nuclear arms."[3] But this was not the prelude to an integrated arms control proposal encompassing nonproliferation; rather, it heralded a call for all nuclear suppliers to adopt comprehensive safeguards as a condition of their nuclear exports.

The administration's declared support for nuclear-weapon-free zones in certain regions also implies a linkage between nonproliferation and nuclear arms control and disarmament. As these zones have been conceived, they would further regional as well as global disarmament by averting local nuclear arms races, reassuring the parties against nuclear attack from outside the region, and fostering an atmosphere conducive to general and complete disarmament. Moreover, these zones could promote nonproliferation objectives and thereby complement the NPT at the regional level.

In his July 1981 nonproliferation statement, the president said the United States continues to support adherence to the Treaty of Tlatelolco (which established a denuclearized zone in Latin America) by those countries in the region that had not yet accepted its provisions. In addition, noted Reagan, he would encourage Senate consent to ratification of Protocol I to the Treaty of Tlatelolco, which has since been ratified.

The administration has also indicated support for the creation of nuclear-weapon-free zones in South Asia and the Middle East. In South Asia, the United States has favored a denuclearized zone since 1977. Although the administration remains supportive of such a zone in principle, there has been no indication of action to achieve this objective. As for the Middle East, the United States has voted since 1974 in favor of UN resolutions recommending the creation of a denuclearized zone in the region but has done little more. Nonetheless, on 13 August 1981, Eugene Rostow, then director of the Arms Control and Disarmament Agency (ACDA), called for the establishment of a nuclear-weapon-free zone in the Middle East modeled on the Latin American zone. (This followed the Israeli raid on Iraq's research reactor in June 1981.) No meaningful action has so far been taken, and Rostow's initiative has faded from the scene.

While the administration has declared support for denuclearized zones in

South Asia and the Middle East, it has rejected in principle the Nordic and Central European nuclear-weapon-free zones proposed by the Scandinavians and the Soviets in recent years. In the administration's view, they would disrupt the superpower balance in Europe and around the world.

In addition to the linkage of nonproliferation and nuclear disarmament that can reasonably be inferred from certain elements of its nonproliferation policy, the Reagan administration has on occasion acknowledged the connections between these modes of controlling nuclear arms. Notably, in his address to the UN General Assembly's Special Session on Disarmament on 17 June 1982, Reagan recalled that since the end of World War II the United States has been the leader in serious arms control and disarmament proposals, among them the NPT. According to the president, "the United States played a major role in this key effort to prevent the spread of nuclear explosives and to provide for international safeguards on civil nuclear activities. My country remains deeply committed to these objectives today, and to strengthening the nonproliferation framework. This is essential to international security."[4] Although the president included nonproliferation in the context of arms control in his speech, initiatives to prevent further proliferation had not found their way into his "agenda for peace," the "broad-based comprehensive series of [arms control] proposals to reduce the risk of war" that had been put forward by Washington in the preceding months.[5]

While elements of the Reagan nonproliferation policy have implied a link between preventing the spread of nuclear weapons to countries that do not now have them and controlling or reducing the nuclear arsenals of the weapon states, the administration has not formally acknowedged this linkage. Changes in international relations may force it to review its policy in this area. East-West relations have deteriorated to a very low point, and domestic and international concern about the nuclear arms race and the prospects of nuclear war remains high. In these circumstances, it is virtually inevitable that the risk of nuclear weapons spreading to states that do not now possess them will be viewed with growing concern, and the absence of progress on nuclear arms control may well affect the administration's capacity to achieve its nonproliferation objectives.

Progress on nuclear arms control will not be achieved easily. Suspicions about the results of previous arms control negotiations, evidence of certain or likely Soviet noncompliance with past arms control agreements, and difficult and contentious verification issues associated with new nuclear systems have led the administration to adopt a cautious approach to arms control. It has enunciated, as "essential principles guiding the U.S. approach," the pursuit of agreements that will enhance security while reducing the risks of war; of substantial, mutual reductions of weapons and forces to equal levels; of provisions for effective verification; and of reliable instruments to deal with issues of compliance. These principles were in evidence in the president's proposal to renegotiate the verification provisions of the pending Threshold Test Ban Treaty (TTBT) and the Peaceful Nuclear Explosions Treaty (PNET). As well, they were evident in the administration's review of arms control policy that preceded the opening of the INF and strategic arms reduction (START) negotiations.

However sound in principle, the administration's approach has been questioned in the United States and abroad. The motives behind administration concerns about verifying nuclear test bans were viewed suspiciously, and the early INF and START proposals were widely perceived to be unnegotiable and reactive. Critics in the United States and Europe charged that it was only in response to domestic and international events that the Reagan administration appeared to moderate its opinions and publicize its own nuclear arms control initiatives. These critics noted that the administration announced its "zero-option" negotiating position on INF and entered into negotiations with the Soviets only after the European unilateral disarmament movement had demonstrated its strength in the autumn of 1981. In similar fashion, they charged, the administration announced its START proposal and began negotiations only after the bilateral-freeze movement began to manifest power and political potential throughout the United States and to receive mounting congressional support. The administration has denied that its arms control approach has been reactive. Rather, it has portrayed its INF and START initiatives as resulting from a careful preparatory review of arms control policy and the need to ensure that its "essential principles" were incorporated in its negotiating positions.

Despite its entry into arms control negotiations in 1981 and 1982, the Reagan administration continued to be suspected in Europe and at home of a lukewarm commitment to arms control and disarmament. These suspicions were intensified by administration decisions to proceed with preexisting commitments to deploy new nuclear weapon systems, notably Pershing II and MX, which were portrayed as dangerous and destabilizing, and by "saber-rattling" statements by high-level officials. Further, the administration was portrayed by some elements of the media as intransigent during early rounds of the INF and START negotiations, which probably further diminished the credibility of its commitment to arms control. Other words and actions probably worsened the U.S. position in the eyes of Americans and Europeans alike. Notably, concerns about the administration's arms control policy were intensified by the publicity surrounding the dismissal of ACDA Director Eugene Rostow and the nomination of Kenneth Adelman to replace him.

Administration efforts in 1983 and 1984 to develop a bipartisan arms control policy on the basis of the recommendations of the President's Commission on Strategic Forces (Scowcroft Commission) and the "build-down" concept developed in cooperation with the congressional "gang of six" have somewhat ameliorated suspicions of the administration's arms control commitment. In the aftermath of the Korean Airlines incident and the Soviet withdrawal from the START and INF talks, public opinion in the United States and Western Europe has shifted to some extent toward the U.S. position. But, as recent congressional debates and voting on MX funding indicate, the administration is still viewed with considerable skepticism. As the stalemate in Geneva persists, further critiques of current U.S. arms control policy are to be expected, as are increased proliferation concerns.

Modernizing Nuclear Arms

The ongoing modernization of U.S. nuclear arms is central to the Reagan defense policy and is defended as necessary to replace aging weapons and to counter the threat of growing Soviet nuclear forces. It is also being pursued as the prerequisite to any serious Soviet interest in negotiations on sharply reducing or eliminating intermediate-range and strategic nuclear forces. Critics argue, however, that the pursuit of U.S. security through nuclear arms modernization could actually endanger U.S. security by increasing the risks of proliferation.

By 1980, according to the Reagan administration, the strategic balance was shifting to the Soviet advantage. The administration argued that the United States was confronted with a "window of vulnerability" during which the Minuteman intercontinental ballistic missile (ICBM) force would be vulnerable to a Soviet first strike. In these circumstances, the deterrent value of the U.S. strategic forces was seen to be eroding. In the European theater, moreover, the deployment of Soviet SS-20 intermediate-range ballistic missiles targeted on Europe appeared to be diminishing the deterrent value of NATO forces and the credibility of NATO nuclear strategy. The administration's response to these perceived dangers was to proceed with a comprehensive program for modernizing U.S. strategic and NATO theater-nuclear forces.

In accordance with the December 1979 NATO dual-track decision, and in the absence of an INF arms control agreement to eliminate SS-20s, NATO is modernizing its long-range theater-nuclear forces by deploying 464 Tomahawk ground-launched cruise missiles and 108 Pershing II ballistic missiles in Western Europe. Because there had been no agreement in U.S.-Soviet INF negotiations when the Soviets withdrew in late 1983, initial deployment was begun in the FRG, Italy, and the United Kingdom. As for U.S. strategic forces, Reagan announced a comprehensive program for modernizing the U.S. strategic triad on 2 October 1981. To be funded over six years at a cost of more than $180 billion in 1982 dollars, this program has several mutually reinforcing elements: modernization of the strategic bomber force through deployment of B-1B bombers by the mid-1980s, and the deployment of cruise missiles on B-52Gs and B-52Hs; a phased introduction of land-based MX "Peacekeeper" missiles; deployment of Trident II D-5 submarine-launched ballistic missiles; strengthening of communications and control systems by improving Pave Paws surveillance radars, hardening existing E-4B and EC-135 command posts, and instituting other measures; and improvements to strategic air defenses. Although the MX has been threatened by congressional budgetary actions, it has survived so far. Thus, the key elements of the administration's program have been relatively unaffected by the annual budget ritual, and they were generally reaffirmed by the Scowcroft Commission report of 6 April 1983. The Commission recommended a strategic modernization program that included deployment of one hundred MX ICBMs in existing silos and development of a small, single-warhead ICBM.

Even though the administration holds that modernizing U.S. nuclear forces is necessary to bring the Soviets to the table and force them to negotiate seriously, and offered the vision of an ultimate defense against nuclear-armed ballistic missiles in the president's televised "Star Wars" speech, its proposed modernization of strategic and theater-nuclear forces has been controversial in the United States and abroad. If nuclear systems like the Pershing II and the Peacekeeper continue to survive congressional and public onslaughts and are not restrained or reduced by successful arms control agreements, they could indirectly increase the risks of further horizontal proliferation. Although prudence might suggest their necessity for the defense of the United States and its allies in light of the incessant buildup of Soviet nuclear forces over the past decade, programs for the modernization of strategic and theater-nuclear forces publicly reemphasize that the security of the United States depends upon its arsenal of nuclear weapons. The U.S. nuclear deterrent, through its extension to our allies, has proven to be an effective nonproliferation instrument. However, if the arms race continues unabated, and other non-nuclear-weapon states are unable to obtain what they perceive to be adequate security assurances from the United States and other nuclear-weapon states, the prospect of near-nuclear countries opting for nuclear weapons will become increasingly likely. Successful arms control agreements appear to offer the best hope of resolving this dilemma—of preserving strategic stability while stemming proliferation—in the long term.

Other administration decisions designed to ensure U.S. national security could also affect the conduct of U.S. nonproliferation policy. One such decision involved a contingency plan to provide for the increasing plutonium requirements of the nuclear weapons programs the administration is championing. In March 1981, the Department of Energy informed the House Armed Services Committee that successful development of an advanced laser technique for refining plutonium could allow approximately 70,000 kilograms of plutonium now contained in commercial spent fuel to be used for weapons. In September 1981, the secretary of energy informed the department's Energy Research Advisory Board that applications of this laser isotope separation (LIS) technique would enable plutonium from commercial spent fuel to be used both for U.S. weapons and breeder-reactor programs.

The secretary's statement provoked critical domestic and international reactions. Concern was expressed that use of the LIS technique would effectively obliterate the boundary established between the peaceful atom and the military atom. Although administration officials later emphasized that LIS is only in contingency planning, and that other sources of weapons-grade plutonium are available, congressional concern resulted in an amendment to the Nuclear Regulatory Commission (NRC) authorization for 1981 and 1982 that prohibits the NRC from licensing transfers of commercial spent fuel or plutonium to DOE for weapons purposes. At present, there is apparently no administration plan to use LIS to enable commercial spent fuel to be used in U.S. weapons programs. Together with the statutory ban, this fact serves to limit possible damage to U.S. nonproliferation policy.

The Reagan administration's decisions in 1982 not to negotiate a Comprehensive Test Ban Treaty (CTBT) and not to seek ratification of the Threshold Test Ban Treaty or the Peaceful Nuclear Explosions Treaty may raise similar questions. These decisions were probably driven by the need for further nuclear weapons testing to ensure an effective nuclear deterrent. However desirable for the maintenance and further development of U.S. nuclear forces, these decisions could also inhibit the effectiveness of U.S. nonproliferation initiatives.

The administration believes that neither the PNET nor TTBT, as negotiated, contains adequate verification provisions and has proposed to the Soviets that both treaties be renegotiated. And, even though the administration has stated publicly that it remains committed to a comprehensive test ban as "a long-term U.S. goal,"[6] it is currently unwilling to forgo nuclear testing, recognizing the importance of testing for the ongoing nuclear force modernization and believing it to be vital to the security of the United States.

The administration's approach to nuclear testing has been criticized for several reasons, among them its potential effect on the international nonproliferation regime. A treaty banning peaceful nuclear explosions (PNEs), if it could be adequately verified, could have benefits for a nonproliferation regime in which there is political ambiguity about PNEs, which are technically indistinguishable from military explosions. And, a verifiable and fully observed comprehensive test ban might reinforce the NPT regime by indicating the good faith of the nuclear-weapon states in fulfilling the preambular pledge and their Article VI obligations. It could provide a useful instrument for preventing any non-nuclear-weapon states that are contemplating nuclear weapon programs from detonating explosive devices. However, it must be recognized that a comprehensive test ban is not a substitute for arms reductions. Nor would it necessarily prevent proliferation, even though it could in principle make the acquisition of nuclear weapons by states that do not possess them more costly in economic and political terms.

U.S. Security Dilemmas

On the basis of the NPT ''bargain,'' the nuclear haves and have-nots were expected to work toward a world without nuclear weapons. From the vantage point of the early 1980s, however, many non-nuclear-weapon states argue that the nuclear-weapon states have not kept their part of the deal and have thereby endangered the entire NPT regime. If this danger has frequently been exaggerated for political reasons, it is nonetheless real, and it poses dilemmas for the pursuit of U.S. security interests in the 1980s. Measures necessary to ensure the deterrent value of U.S. nuclear forces might have an adverse effect on the achievement of arms control agreements and could also be debilitating to nonproliferation efforts. A diminished U.S. capacity to prevent further proliferation and to realize limitations or reductions of nuclear arms, however, could decrease U.S. security. On the other hand, implementation of nuclear force reductions through arms control agreements with the Soviet Union could decrease the perceived value of U.S. security assurances, thereby increasing the insecurity of certain allies and their real or imagined need to develop nuclear arsenals.

To some extent, U.S. national security policy will have to adapt to these dilemmas. Clearly, necessary nuclear arms modernizations should not be precluded merely because they could create incentives for further proliferation. Nor should a comprehensive test ban be negotiated because it could inhibit nuclear weapons aspirations among non-nuclear-weapon states, if it entails unreasonable risks to the U.S. nuclear deterrent and, thereby, to U.S. national security. It is, of course, possible that our long-term national security interests will necessitate decisions that, in the short term, involve proliferation risks. Indeed, this may be inevitable. Yet, in these and other decisions involving nuclear arms, arms control, and disarmament, the impact on proliferation should be seriously considered. Balance is required, and it is necessary to avoid creating impressions that can only worsen a precarious situation. All in all, if the pursuit of U.S. security interests is not to be paralyzed by the policy dilemmas just discussed, a judicious approach is necessary. Only with a policy approach that recognizes the linkage of arms control and nonproliferation, and addresses this critical link, can the Reagan administration or any other U.S.

administration avoid neglecting or sacrificing some U.S. security interests in the pursuit of others.

Notes

1. Hans Blix, director-general of the International Atomic Energy Agency, statement, Second Session of the United Nations General Assembly Devoted to Disarmament, 16 June 1982.
2. Ronald Reagan, "Statement on United States Nuclear Nonproliferation and Peaceful Nuclear Cooperation Policy," 16 July 1981.
3. Ronald Reagan, address, Los Angeles World Affairs Council, 31 March 1983.
4. Ronald Reagan, statement, Second Session of the United Nations General Assembly Devoted to Disarmament, 17 June 1982.
5. Ibid.
6. *Security and Arms Control: The Search for a More Stable Peace* (Washington, D.C.: U.S. Department of State, Bureau of Public Affairs, June 1983), p. 58.

11

Nuclear Nonproliferation: The Long Haul

Lewis A. Dunn

It is nearly forty years since the successful detonation of the first nuclear explosive at Alamogordo, New Mexico, in July 1945. Since that time, every U.S. administration has been committed to preventing the further spread of nuclear weapons around the globe. This commitment, as the paper in this volume by Ambassador-at-Large for Nonproliferation Richard T. Kennedy, makes clear, is a high priority of the Reagan administration.

The policy of this administration rests upon the recognition that nuclear proliferation would profoundly threaten international stability and global order. Suspicions among traditional rivals would be exacerbated, regional disputes made more complex, and the possibility of local conflict increased. The security and well-being of the United States and its close friends and allies, but also the security and well-being of the countries acquiring these weapons, would be threatened. Indeed, the greatest chance of use of nuclear weapons stems not from the U.S.-Soviet strategic balance but from the possible emergence of small, unstable nuclear arsenals in many regions of the world characterized by crises and periodic military conflict.

Consider the dangers, for example, if either Iran or Iraq had nuclear weapons. For over the years, these countries have been involved in a bloody war of attrition. Recently, Iran resorted to human-wave assaults and there is increasing evidence that Iraq has used chemical weapons. There have been nearly a million casualties on both sides. The chance of either Iran or Iraq's getting nuclear weapons in the foreseeable future is remote, and we continue to work to make it more so. But, if either country had those weapons, there would be great pressures to use them. The dangers of escalation in the region would be increased immeasurably. And there would be a heightened prospect of superpower involvement in the conflict.

Basic United States Policy

Much of the day-to-day activity within the United States government to meet the threat of nuclear proliferation focuses upon immediate problems and developments. For example, in the past several years, the Reagan administration has worked hard to strengthen nuclear supplier constraints by fostering a consensus to tighten the international export control lists for items that could contribute to nuclear weapons development. Policies also have been initiated that should lessen the motivations that can lead a country to acquire nuclear explosives, while important U.S. security ties and alliances have been buttressed. In addition, the administration has endeavored to strengthen International Atomic Energy Agency (IAEA) safeguards, reduce the intrusion of extraneous political issues into the work of the IAEA, bring new countries into the Nonproliferation Treaty (NPT), and make more likely the full entry into force of the Treaty of Tlatelolco in Latin America.

In dealing with these day-to-day problems and issues, the administration has adopted what Ambassador Kennedy has termed a common-sense approach. We have stressed cooperation rather than confrontation in an attempt to generate increased support for strong nonproliferation policies among nations with active nuclear programs. Also, we have sought to avoid the best's becoming the enemy of the good, leading us to sacrifice gains that are attainable in pursuit of those which are not, because of either wishful thinking or a misguided belief that we should have gotten or done more. Most important, the Reagan administration's nuclear common-sense approach has recognized the need to deal with the world as it is rather than as we might like it to be.

For nonproliferation policy to be successful, however, it must look beyond immediate problems and issues to the trends and challenges that will affect our efforts to prevent the spread of nuclear weapons in the coming decades. While prediction is hazarded only with great risk, especially in the nuclear field in which so many diverse forces interact, at least four longer-term problems stand out in the context of future policy: the steady erosion of technical barriers to acquiring nuclear explosives; the emergence of new suppliers; the shift to more advanced nuclear fuel-cycle activities in certain countries; and the need to extend the Nonproliferation Treaty when it comes up for renewal in 1995. How we deal with these challenges will help determine the prospects for nonproliferation over the long haul.

The Erosion of Technical Barriers

A country seeking nuclear weapons must hurdle two main technical barriers. First, it must acquire the necessary nuclear weapons material, whether plutonium or highly enriched uranium. Second, it must design and successfully fabricate a nuclear explosive device. When the United States first set out on the nuclear weapons path nearly forty years ago, crossing these barriers demanded efforts at the forefront of many fields, including physics, chemistry, engineering, explosives, metallurgy, and electronics. In the ensuing decades, however, global economic development has brought more and more countries closer to the level of scientific and industrial capability needed to master this task. Similarly, the spread of the peaceful atom has contributed to a technical understanding of nuclear energy that can be put into military as well as peaceful purposes.

Efforts still are needed—and are under way in cooperation with other nuclear suppliers—to slow this erosion of technical constraints and to put obstacles in the path of a country seeking nuclear explosives. But these measures can only buy time. In some cases, given the very backward state of a country, the time may be measured in decades. In most cases, the time is much shorter. As the process of economic and industrial change continues, more countries will be able to surmount the technical barriers and the amount of time that can be bought will become steadily less. Thus, for the long haul, it is necessary to consider how to use that time wisely.

One important way to use that time is to take measures to reduce specific countries' incentives to acquire nuclear explosives. A strong and credible U.S. alliance system has a central part to play. Throughout the postwar period, U.S. alliances with the countries of Western Europe and with Japan have helped ensure these countries' security and have made it unnecessary for them to think about the acquisition of nuclear weapons. Credible alliance or security ties with South Korea and Taiwan in Northeast Asia also have had a significant nonproliferation payoff. Buttressed support for Pakistan's security still holds out the best chance of convincing that country not to build or test a nuclear explosive. These relations need to be preserved and strengthened in the years ahead.

Though admittedly difficult, steps to reduce regional tensions and foster settlement of local disputes also can lessen the motivations, whether real or imagined, that can move nations toward nuclear explosives. In that regard, the improvement of relations between Egypt and Israel brought about in the late 1970s by the Camp David process served nonproliferation goals.

We must also use the time available to enhance the international norm against the acquisition of nuclear weapons. By strengthening the norm, many countries' calculations can be indirectly influenced. Past experience demonstrates the norm's gradual emergence. In 1960, after France detonated its first nuclear weapon in the Algerian desert, President de Gaulle immediately telephoned congratulations to the scientists at the site. He lauded their great feat and stressed that France too now had access to the most advanced weapons, as befitted its status as a great power. By contrast, when India detonated a nuclear explosive in the Rajasthan Desert a little more than a decade later in 1974, Prime Minister Indira Gandhi called that blast "a peaceful nuclear explosion." She emphasized the utility of such explosions in building harbors, digging channels, and other excavation operations. The international mood and the expected standard of behavior had changed. It no longer was regarded as legitimate to acquire nuclear weapons, and India sought to sneak into the nuclear weapons club through the back door.

One way, discussed fully later, by which the Reagan administration strives to strengthen the norm against acquisition of nuclear weapons is by working for the Nonproliferation Treaty. That treaty, to which more than 120 countries have adhered, clearly demonstrates the vitality of the nonproliferation norm, for under it, nonnuclear nations have formally and unambiguously renounced the right to acquire nuclear explosives.

The Treaty of Tlatelolco also symbolizes the pervasiveness of the international norm of nonproliferation. Promoted and negotiated by the countries of Latin America, it seeks to create a continent free of nuclear weapons. All but a few Latin American countries have joined, and the five nuclear-weapon states have agreed to Protocol II to the Treaty, which notably prohibits threats or use of their nuclear weapons against Latin American countries that have taken the steps necessary to bring the treaty into force.

Over the next years, the United States and others need to continue efforts to remove the last obstacles to the Treaty of Tlatelolco's becoming fully effective. To that end, President Reagan in 1981 sought and obtained Senate ratification of Protocol I of the treaty, by which outside states with de jure or de facto responsibility for territories within the geographical zone established by the treaty agree to apply its denuclearization provisions to those territories. France's ratification of that protocol, as well as decisions by a few countries in Latin America that have not yet joined the treaty, are the remaining obstacles that need to be overcome.

Successful arms control negotiations aimed at radical reductions in the nuclear arsenals of the United States and the Soviet Union also can contribute to the norm of nonproliferation. For its part, the Reagan administration has made clear to the Soviet Union its readiness to resume the START and INF talks on deep reductions, without preconditions and taking into account respective U.S. and Soviet force structures. But to achieve such reductions, there must be give and take on both sides. Although the reductions would not directly influence the policies of countries that might be thinking about acquiring nuclear explosives, they can help demonstrate a commitment by existing nuclear-weapon states to reduce the role of nuclear weapons in world politics. That would help create a climate in which decisions to acquire nuclear explosives would be more difficult to take and less easy to justify in terms of the "alleged" misdeeds of the existing nuclear-weapon states.

Emerging Nuclear Suppliers

The steady emergence of additional suppliers over the next decade also poses a potential long-term problem for nuclear nonproliferation policy. Argentina, Brazil, India, Israel, South Korea, Spain, South Africa, China, Yugoslavia, and Romania are all increasingly capable of supplying nuclear technology, equipment, and/or materials. These are a diverse group of countries, yet all but one have not adhered to existing multilateral nuclear export controls. (South Africa announced in January 1984 that its nuclear export policies would be "in accordance with the provisions" of the London Nuclear Suppliers Group guidelines. China also indicated that after its admission to the IAEA on 1 January 1984, it would require IAEA safeguards on its new commitments for nuclear exports.)

The prospect of a renegade nuclear supplier has always been a cause for nonproliferation concern. Were these countries to export nuclear material, for example, without requiring the types of safeguards and assurances of peaceful uses that the major suppliers require, that would remove an important political impediment to the misuse of such exports. Similarly, the spread of sensitive nuclear technology, which many of these countries are capable of providing to one degree or another, would make it easier for countries seeking nuclear explosives to move in that direction. More widespread availability of sensitive nuclear technology also would heighten suspicion amongst neighboring countries. And if these new suppliers came to compete seriously for sales with the major nuclear suppliers, that could lead to a gradual undermining of the international system of nuclear controls, for the major suppliers might well be reluctant to continue to require tight safeguards and assurances on their sales, or even to forgo sales of some items in sensitive regions, if new suppliers not abiding by these norms were successful in the competition.

One reason that a new supplier might adopt a less restrained policy would be the need to earn hard currency, whether via nuclear sales or use of such sales as a sweetener for sales of other items. Need for scarce resources, e.g. oil, also could produce a readiness to trim corners. Or a payoff for political support could be involved.

Nonetheless, there are various countervailing considerations that could lead the emerging nuclear suppliers to behave more cautiously as they enter the nuclear supply arena. Some of these countries are parties to the Nonproliferation Treaty and thus are bound by its obligation concerning nuclear supply. Many depend on the existing nuclear suppliers for aid to their own nuclear programs and to their economies, which would be jeopardized by irresponsible behavior. Moreover, the structure of their own nuclear industries suggests that although they could supply certain components or even some types of facilities, they are unlikely to be major competitors with existing suppliers for sales of nuclear power plants. Most lack the ability to export major nuclear power components or reactors and do not have the ability to provide financing for such sales. In addition, prestige considerations might lead them to avoid transfers of sensitive technology in an attempt to maintain technological superiority over other countries. Not least, their own self-interest and security would not be served by a gradual erosion of existing nonproliferation constraints and the further spread of nuclear weapons.

A long-term strategy to deal with the emergence of new suppliers must seek to build on the countervailing pressures and appeal to these countries on the grounds of their own self-interest. Its goal should be to move the new suppliers step by step closer to acceptable nuclear supply norms. As a minimum, the norms should include requiring safeguards on exports, government-to-government assurances of peaceful uses, and assurances of adequate physical security. If possible, a commitment by new suppliers to exercise restraint in the export of sensitive nuclear technology also would be desirable. At the heart of this effort would be bilateral contacts between the existing nuclear suppliers and the emerging suppliers.

U.S. bilateral efforts in this regard already have had some success. Over the past several years, the United States has initiated discussions with some of these emerging suppliers, including Argentina, Brazil, China, South Africa, and Spain. The two sides have exchanged views on the reasons for nuclear export controls and on the general responsibility of nuclear suppliers. The United States has encouraged new suppliers to adopt tighter national control systems for their nuclear exports and has explained U.S. procedures and processes—as well as the benefits of adequate controls. Despite criticism by some of these new suppliers of U.S. controls over exports to them, the discussions have met with some success. The countries have been receptive to the argument that their security would be served by ensuring that their own nuclear exports not contribute to proliferation. They also have been interested in the types of measures that make up an effective system of export controls.

These U.S. efforts need to continue in the coming years, and to be supplemented by contacts by other suppliers with emerging suppliers. In addition, the United States should work to help these countries identify the nuclear-related articles that they produce that could be of assistance to a country's nuclear explosive program. Where appropriate, sharing of information on specific nonproliferation problems also can help to convince a country to cooperate in controlling dangerous exports.

The Committee on Assurances of Supply (CAS) established by the IAEA in 1980 might provide one forum for dialogue on nuclear supply norms. Created in partial reaction to the Nuclear Suppliers Group, CAS includes emerging supplier nations, recipients, and the existing suppliers. Its discussion of "principles" that should govern nuclear trade could be used to encourage the new suppliers to move closer to the accepted norms of international nuclear commerce. Similarly, the case for rigorous supply standards needs to be made in the discussions of the 1986 UN Conference on the Peaceful Uses of Nuclear Energy (PUNE). But any agreement in these forums will stop short of the guidelines adopted by the London Nuclear Suppliers Group.

In regard to how to deal with the longer-term problem of new suppliers, one final point is in order. International norms for nuclear supply have gradually evolved over the past decades. The existing suppliers learned from experience that improved procedures and controls were needed to ensure that their peaceful nuclear dealings did not contribute to military programs. The system that came about works reasonably well but can still be strengthened. It is important that the existing international norm not be eroded in the process of seeking consensus with emerging suppliers. Such a lowest common denominator would equally threaten our longer-term nonproliferation goals.

Advanced Nuclear Fuel-Cycle Activities

Several countries with mature nuclear programs are likely to move in the coming decades toward more advanced fuel-cycle activities involving the use of civil plutonium as a fuel. This will include breeder reactor research and development, the deployment of prototype breeders and other advanced reactors, and some recycling of mixed plutonium-uranium fuel in light-water reactors (LWRs). Because plutonium is a weapons-usable material, its use must be carefully assessed and controlled. Nonetheless, the current slowdown in the shift to more advanced fuel-cycle programs provides breathing space to design ways to insure that use of plutonium as a fuel in the civil sector does not add to the risk of nuclear proliferation and threaten international security.

A long-term approach to this problem must begin from a recognition that it is neither desirable nor feasible to prevent the use of plutonium as a fuel in all countries. Several close U.S. allies, including Japan and members of the European Community, have already made sizable financial commitments to breeder reactor programs, and are evaluating recycling plutonium in light-water reactors. Use of plutonium under appropriate controls in these countries with advanced nuclear programs does not pose a proliferation risk. Nor would it serve U.S. nonproliferation goals to attempt to force the countries to abandon activities that they consider important for their own energy security. Such futile pressure from the United States would only make it more difficult to obtain their cooperation in the nonproliferation area.

At the same time, it is necessary to recognize that in other situations—where a country may not be as politically stable and fundamentally committed against the development of nuclear weapons, or is in an unstable region of tension—the use of plutonium would pose a proliferation risk. Here, it is necessary to try to convince the country not to use plutonium as a fuel. To that end, the United States can and will bring to bear its political and economic influence, as well as make use of the legal controls that it has over the reprocessing of U.S.-origin material. But it also must seek ways to ensure that such a country still can have the benefits of peaceful nuclear energy. And to the extent that pressures to move toward reprocessing and the use of plutonium rest upon the need to find a solution to spent-fuel management, steps need to be taken to provide an alternative.

More generally, prudence suggests trying to restrict the processing, storage, and use of plutonium to as few sites as possible. This will lessen the problems of physical security. The United States also will continue to work directly with other countries to strengthen the international standards for physical protection and international transportation of sensitive nuclear material, and ensure the standards' prompt implementation. In particular, agreement has now been reached internationally on a convention on the physical protection of nuclear material, and we are encouraging all countries to follow us in ratifying it and taking steps to put it into effect.

Additionally, agreement also is needed on the design and implementation of safeguards for large commercial reprocessing plants and bulk-handling facilities. The matter of safeguards was studied by the International Nuclear Fuel Cycle Evaluation and by an IAEA advisory group; neither reached agreement on a preferred safeguards approach. The Reagan administration has begun to forge an international consensus on an effective safeguards approach for these facilities, using the time made available by the slowdown of advanced nuclear fuel-cycle activities. Bilateral discussions among key technology holders are now under way, and can be followed by talks involving the IAEA. It is none too soon to determine how many new IAEA inspectors, what types of new equipment, and what other procedural, budgetary, and management changes would be necessary for the IAEA to safeguard these advanced fuel-cycle activities.

For some countries, pressures to use plutonium as a fuel do not stem from a commitment to the development of the breeder reactor or other advanced fuel-cycle activities to gain enhanced energy independence. Previously, these countries sent spent fuel abroad for reprocessing as a waste-management measure, but now they are paying increasingly expensive fees to store the separated plutonium, and the prospect of using the plutonium as fuel in their existing LWRs is becoming more attractive. This is so despite the fact that, at least initially, an assessment of economic benefits and costs probably would not have justified a decision to recycle plutonium. Consequently, a final part of a long-term strategy would be to develop, where appropriate, alternative spent-fuel and waste-management options, which would lessen the need for many countries to choose to recycle plutonium simply because it was the only available (if uneconomic) approach to disposing of spent fuel.

Preserving and Extending the Nonproliferation Treaty

The Nonproliferation Treaty, as mentioned above, is one of the cornerstones of international efforts to prevent the spread of nuclear explosives. Article X provides, however, that twenty-five years after the treaty's entry into force a conference shall be convened to decide whether it shall continue in force indefinitely, or whether it shall be extended for a fixed period or periods. Thus, in 1995 the parties to the treaty will have to decide its fate. We need to begin thinking about how to ensure a positive decision to maintain the stability of this crucial international security measure.

A key part of U.S. strategy to preserve the NPT must be persistent and persuasive efforts to convince all parties of the importance of the security benefits it provides. For several reasons, were the treaty regime to collapse, a key impediment to the further spread of nuclear weapons would be lost. Political pressures not to acquire nuclear weapons would be reduced, for a major legal element establishing the international nonproliferation norm would have been weakened. Similarly, without this confidence-building institution, heightened suspicions about neighboring countries' intentions could set in motion steps toward obtaining explosives. And without the nuclear supply obligations of the treaty, it would be harder to persuade other suppliers to restrain potentially dangerous exports.

Moves to strengthen the benefits of the NPT in terms of access to peaceful nuclear technology and equipment are also part of a long-run strategy. Although the overall record of the major nuclear suppliers in supporting the peaceful uses of nuclear energy is a very good one, it still can be improved. And the United States is exploring ways to provide greater preference in peaceful nuclear dealings with parties to the treaty. For example, heightened preference could be provided by other countries, as the United States now does, in making available fellowships and training under the IAEA. More broadly, the United States is seeking closer bilateral nuclear ties with key nonaligned parties to the treaty, helping them with both power and nonpower applications of nuclear energy. Other countries have been encouraged to do so as well. And agreement among the major nuclear suppliers that comprehensive safeguards should be a necessary condition of significant, new supply, as proposed by President Reagan, would provide a clear means for assuring that nonparties receive less favorable treatment than do nations that have not accepted the important commitments embodied in the treaty.

Under Article VI of the NPT, the parties pledge "to pursue negotiations in good faith on effective measures relating to cessation of the nuclear arms race.'' But many non-nuclear-weapon states have been critical of the limited success of those efforts and have questioned the concrete arms control value of the treaty. Thus, over the longer term, the type of progress described above in arms control involving the United States and the Soviet Union also would help the survival of the treaty after 1995.

Intensified work is needed as well to persuade the countries still remaining outside the NPT to join. Here we can identify two categories: first, what we may call the hard-line holdouts, such as Israel, South Africa, Argentina, and others; second, a group comprising possible targets of opportunity. While continuing to emphasize the importance of treaty adherence even with the former countries, we should focus on and are focusing more attention on the latter countries, which might be prepared to join the treaty, arguing that adherence will serve their long-term security interests and provide other benefits. And to the extent that the treaty comes closer to being universally accepted, momentum is added to the norm of nonproliferation.

But before we can face the problems of preserving the NPT when it comes up for renewal in 1995, we must transit the period in between. In particular, in 1985 and most probably again in 1990, there will be international conferences to review its implementation. Planning already is well under way within the United States for the 1985 review conference. Because the outcome of the conference is likely to influence the vitality of the NPT throughout the decade, it is important to demonstrate that it has broad support among its many parties. To achieve that outcome, it will be necessary to defend the implementation of specific articles of the treaty, for example, the commitment of the parties to facilitate the fullest possible exchange of peaceful nuclear energy (Article IV) and to engage in good faith arms control negotiations (Article VI). But most of all it will require a recognition on the part of the participants that in the final analysis and whatever its shortcomings, the Nonprolifreation Treaty is a critical instrument of international security. Put simply, without it, the security of all countries would be lessened.

If we are to achieve our nonproliferation objectives over the long haul, we shall have to design and implement effective policies to deal with the types of problems that have been discussed in this paper. Some of these problems are technical in nature; some, political. How well we deal with these longer-term developments will go far to determine the prospects for avoiding the spread of nuclear weapons in the decades ahead.

12

To Manage Is Human, To Prevent Is Divine

Joseph S. Nye, Jr.

Twenty years ago, John F. Kennedy saw the possibility of a world in the 1970s with fifteen to twenty-five nuclear weapons states, a situation he regarded as "the greatest possible danger." Instead, the 1970s closed with five declared weapons states, one state that had launched a "peaceful nuclear explosion," and one or two that were believed to be just below the explosion threshold. Since nuclear weaponry is a forty-year-old technology, what is surprising is not that it has spread, but that it has not spread further.

Recently, there has been increasing concern about the apparent slackening of U.S. efforts to slow and manage nuclear proliferation. In the view of the London *Economist*, for example, the Reagan administration's policy looks less like a show of sensible flexibility than like a chipping away at the foundations of the whole international effort to curb nuclear proliferation. In comparison to the Carter administration, the priority certainly seems lower. There have been few presidential statements or initiatives; in addition, some export restrictions have been relaxed, hard cases like South Africa or Argentina have been treated more leniently, and there has been an uneconomic but potentially dangerous promotion of plutonium fuels.

The Reagan administration, to be fair, still follows the general policy that has characterized previous administrations, but it is like a train that follows only the main tracks, with little steam in the engine and subject to frequent, if minor, derailments. Any American government that wants to slow the spread of nuclear weapons in this decade is going to have to deal with the major political problems I have identified and, above all, place a higher priority upon the proliferation problem.

If one specifies a goal of reducing the rate and degree of proliferation in order to manage its destabilizing effects and reduce the prospects of nuclear use, then there are many promising tasks for nonproliferation policy. Even if one were to accept the sanguine view that nuclear proliferation may not be destabilizing in all cases, the rate of proliferation affects the likelihood of destabilizing effects. Sensible policy, moreover, must hedge against potentially large downside risks.

Proliferation is sometimes conceived of in simple terms as a single explosion. Indeed, that concept is enshrined in the Nonproliferation Treaty (NPT). But it can also be conceptualized as analogous to a staircase with many steps before and after a first nuclear test. A first explosion is politically important as a key landing in the staircase, but militarily a single crude explosive device does not bring entry into a meaningful "nuclear club." The very idea of a nuclear club is misleading. The difference between a single crude device and a modern nuclear arsenal is as stark as the difference between having an apple and having an orchard.

There are many reasons why this is so, including the restrictive policies of the weapons states, the calculated self-interest of many nonweapons states in forgoing nuclear weapons, and the development of an international regime of treaties, rules, and procedures that establishes a general presumption against proliferation. The main norms and practices of this regime are found in the NPT and in its regional counterpart trying to work toward a nonnuclear Latin America; in the safeguards, rules, and procedures of the International Atomic Energy Agency (IAEA); as well as in various UN resolutions. While there are a few important exceptions, the great majority of states adhere to at least part of this set of norms.

In the early 1970s, there was a degree of complacency about this nonproliferation regime. That complacency was shattered in 1974 by the Indian explosion of a "peaceful nuclear device," using plutonium derived from a Canadian-supplied research reactor, and by the oil crisis, which had led to a sudden surge of exaggerated expectations about the importance of nuclear energy, including fears that uranium supplies would be exhausted. Nations developed plans for early commercial use of plutonium fuels, and some (such as Korea and Pakistan) arranged to import allegedly commercial reprocessing plants for what were later disclosed to be nuclear explosives programs. Typical projections for the 1980s from this period saw eight reactors in Bangladesh and thirty to forty countries using plutonium fuels by the end of the decade. With this challenge to the nonproliferation regime, it is not surprising that policy responses in the late 1970s, such as those from the Nuclear Suppliers Group and INFCE (International Nuclear Fuel Cycle Evaluation) focused on fuel-cycle issues.

Some of the fuel-cycle issues debated so heatedly in the 1970s have now been resolved by experience, economic trends, and the conclusions of INFCE. For example, the argument that no state would find it rational to try misusing a fuel-cycle facility rather than build a dedicated facility has been disproven by Korea's efforts in the early 1970s and by more recent experience with Pakistan. The view that shortages of uranium would force early use of plutonium has succumbed to more realistic economic projections. The view that nuclear energy would provide energy security has also been belied by reality and better analysis: the great threats to energy security in the 1980s are from political interruptions of Persian Gulf oil, for which the appropriate answer is emergency stockpiles, conservation, and coal, not nuclear plants with ten-year lead times. Moreover, in light of economic experience, the optimistic projections about nuclear energy in developing countries have also had to be toned down for most countries. Of sixteen less-developed countries currently operating reactors, only a half-dozen have significant power programs. Ironically, the early pronouncements of the Reagan administration seem to have been a fading echo of the 1970s debate, rather than the harbinger of the 1980s. And to a considerable extent, the rhetoric succumbed to reality. Public and congressional opinion soon brought the administration back to the mainstream that has characterized U.S. policy since 1975.

Beyond the Fuel Cycle

The nonproliferation problems of the 1980s are more likely to have a political cast and to require political solutions. Fuel-cycle issues will still be important, but the fuel cycle is only one of six major proliferation-management problems that I foresee for this decade.

First, it will be important to keep fuel-cycle questions in a reasonable perspective. The fuel cycle is neither the key to our problems nor irrelevant. Abolishing nuclear energy or nuclear exports would not solve the nuclear proliferation problem, for there are other paths to the bomb. And nuclear supply can provide important leverage. In this sense, the administration's rhetoric about being a reliable supplier makes some sense. But it will backfire unless an effort is made to get other suppliers to help close the loopholes in the export system. Important steps remain to be taken, such as improvement of IAEA safeguards, full-scope safeguards (which means refusal to ship technology and materials to countries with unsafeguarded facilities), special arrangements for managing plutonium and highly enriched uranium, and international provisions for spent-fuel storage.

A second problem is one of priority. Nonproliferation is not a foreign policy, it is part of a foreign policy; and foreign policy always involves the adjustment of partly conflicting objectives in order to achieve as much as possible, within the constraints of a disorderly world. One effect of the attention given to proliferation in the late 1970s was to raise the priority of the issue for a number of governments. The Reagan administration's emphasis on East-

West conflict has led it to neglect areas of potential cooperation with the Soviet Union on nonproliferation. Some skeptics have urged a lowering of the priority given to nonproliferation on the grounds that its negative effects are exaggerated. Just as nuclear weapons have prompted prudence in U.S.-Soviet relations, it is argued, so may nuclear weapons stabilize regional balances. If political conditions were similar, this might be true. But the transferability of prudence assumes governments with stable command-and-control systems, an absence of fierce civil or territorial wars, and discipline over the temptation to make preemptive strikes during the early stages when new nuclear weapons capabilities are soft and vulnerable. Such assumptions are unrealistic in many parts of the world. Indeed, rather than enhancing a state's security, the first effects of acquiring new nuclear capability in many circumstances may be to increase the state's vulnerability and insecurity. The Israeli attack on Iraq's reactor has turned this theoretical point into a reality, and has proved to be an important learning experience in the administration's movement from domestic campaign rhetoric to international reality.

Third, even if there is a high priority given to nonproliferation, difficult policy choices remain concerning the rate and degree of proliferation. As technology spreads and proliferation occurs, we will have to direct more attention to these questions of advanced proliferation. Controls on information about laser fusion devices, technology having advanced weapons uses, as well as space launchers and other delivery systems will require more systematic analysis. Formulation of sanctions that deter a quickening rate while trying to prevent further development after a first explosion will be a delicate balancing act. Such steps can inhibit the development of nuclear-warfighting capabilities and thermonuclear devices.

Fourth, there is the problem of the way international rules and structures can have a net strengthening or weakening effect on each other. In one direction, the nonproliferation regime interacts with other nuclear weapons and arms control regimes; in another, it interacts with international energy and economic regimes. A successful nonproliferation policy in the 1980s will require attention to the connections in both directions.

To profess indifference to the superpower nuclear arms relationship, in particular the U.S.-Soviet negotiations, can weaken the nonproliferation regime. For one thing, a disdain for arms control institutions and for the concerns expressed by nonweapon states can exacerbate the central dilemma in nonproliferation policy—namely, the claim by less-developed countries that the "nuclear club" discriminates against them. The cancellation of negotiations on a comprehensive test ban was unfortunate in this regard. Also, although Reagan doctrines and deployments that stress the usefulness of nuclear weapons in warfighting situations may help make deterrence more credible, they also tend to make nuclear weapons look more attractive to others. If states that have eschewed nuclear weapons see those weapons treated increasingly like conventional defensive weapons, they may well reconsider their original decision.

In the realm of energy and economic regimes, a forthcoming posture on energy and technology transfer, including the development of nonnuclear energy alternatives and other measures to deal with energy insecurity, can help take the edge off confrontations that might otherwise generate a greed for "nuclear club" status and attention rather than security. Yet, this has not been a priority area for the Reagan administration.

A fifth problem has to do with special efforts required at the regional level. One example is the need to complete the Treaty of Tlatelolco (which establishes a nuclear-free zone in Latin America) by obtaining Argentine and Cuban ratification. This might require Soviet help. New measures will be needed for such areas as South Asia or the Middle East, where events have progressed further than in Latin America. A nonexplosion zone could be a useful step. Given the hostility among the parties in the Middle East and their refusal to talk directly with each other, the obstacles are enormous. On the other hand, the idea of developing an additional level of restraint in the Middle East makes sense. One way to do this would be to generalize the existing Israeli statement that they will not be the first to introduce nuclear weapons in the Middle East. In the absence of an agreement among the local states to negotiate, this might be accomplished by having the two superpowers offer a guarantee of no nuclear attack against any state that agrees with the superpowers not to be the first to introduce nuclear weapons into the region (verified by a no-explosion pledge). In other words, the agreement would be between the separate parties in the Middle East, on the one hand, and the superpowers on the other. The *quid pro quo* would be the superpower nonattack guarantee. While this would take some amount of superpower coordination, it is one way of approaching a Middle East nuclear-weapon-free zone in a situation where the local parties are unable or unwilling to talk to one another. A similar plan might be tried in South Asia.

Finally, and perhaps most important, there is the problem of organizing sanctions against proliferators. From time to time, it has been argued that if there is a violation of IAEA safeguards or if there is another explosion of a nuclear device, the reaction of other nations—particularly the superpowers—will be critical. The IAEA safeguards system is like a burglar alarm: if the alarm works but the police do not react, then the system will have little deterrent effect in the future. Yet, this is the sort of situation in which nuclear exporters might seek commercial advantage: each superpower might be tempted to seek separate political advantage by limiting the extent of its reaction against the new proliferator. The mildness of the initial U.S. and Soviet reactions to the 1974 Indian explosion is a case in point. While in these times of hostility in overall U.S.-Soviet relations this may be the most difficult area in which to achieve cooperation, it is nonetheless vitally important to do so. Given technological spread, proliferation will be more feasible over time. Proliferation must remain politically costly to the proliferator if we are to preserve a regime that reduces costs to the common interest.

Managing Proliferation

Over the past three decades, nuclear technology has spread to more than two score nations, yet only a small fraction have chosen to develop nuclear weaponry. Can this situation last? Obviously there will be changes in political and technical trends. But the prospects that proliferation may be destabilizing in many instances, that nuclear weapons need not enhance the security position of states, and that the superpowers cannot fully escape the effects of proliferation provides the common international interest upon which the nonproliferation regime is based. Under such conditions, some inequality in weaponry is acceptable to most states because the alternative—anarchic equality—is more dangerous.

Realistically, an international regime does not require perfect adherence in order to have a significant constraining effect, any more than domestic laws require an absolute end to deviant behavior in order to be effective. Nevertheless, there is a point beyond which violations do lead to the breakdown of constraints. In international politics, the police function is traditionally the domain of the great powers. If they should become diverted by other issues, however, there is a danger that the gradual historical curve of proliferation could approach such a tipping point.

There is no simple solution to the political problem of proliferation. But political wisdom begins with efforts to maintain the existing regime and the presumption against proliferation. In this regard, the Reagan administration has hewed to the previous main lines of American policy. Some critics find it fashionable to talk about "managing proliferation." But proliferation management requires a strategy for prevention—a plan for dealing with the steps before, not just after, a nuclear explosion. Without some prevention, the task of management may become untenable. An effective nonproliferation policy is not easy to design or implement, but we cannot live without one.

About the Contributors

Warren H. Donnelly is a senior specialist in the Congressional Research Service of the Library of Congress. He came to the Library in 1965 after having worked in the Atomic Energy Commission from 1954 to 1963 in its New York Operations Office in technical administration, and from 1963 to 1965 in its Washington headquarters in industrial liaison. At the Library he had a principal part in drafting a report on the Office of Science and Technology and others dealing with Congressional actions affecting science and technology, voluntary industrial standards, and commercial nuclear power in Europe. In 1973 he was appointed a CRS senior specialist in energy.

Lewis A. Dunn is assistant director for nuclear and weapons control of the U.S. Arms Control and Disarmament Agency. Before assuming his present position, he served as counselor to Ambassador-at-Large Richard T. Kennedy. Previously, he was special assistant for nuclear affairs to the under secretary of state for management in 1981-82; on the professional staff of the Hudson Institute in 1974-81, also serving as project leader from 1976 to 1981; and a member of the Department of Political Science at Kenyon College from 1969 to 1974.

John Maxwell Hamilton has worked as foreign correspondent as well as on the staff of the U.S. House Foreign Affairs Committee.

Rodney W. Jones is a senior fellow and director of nuclear policy studies at the Center for Strategic and International Studies, Georgetown University. Before coming to CSIS he was associate professor at Columbia University in the Department of Political Science and Institute of War and Peace Studies. He held an international affairs fellowship from the Council on Foreign Relations with an assignment in the State Department's Bureau of Politico-Military Affairs.

Richard T. Kennedy serves as special adviser to the secretary of state on nonproliferation policy and nuclear energy affairs and coordinator and director of U.S. nonproliferation efforts. Ambassador-at-Large Kennedy is also U.S. representative to the International Atomic Energy Agency. From 1975 to 1980 he was commissioner of the U.S. Nuclear Regulatory Commission.

Richard K. Lester is associate professor of nuclear engineering at the Massachusetts Institute of Technology, where he is also associated with the Center for International Studies. His chief research interests are nuclear-waste management technology, international nuclear trade, and the management of technological innovation.

Joseph S. Nye, Jr. is professor of government at the John F. Kennedy School of Government, Harvard University. From 1977 to 1979 he was deputy to the under secretary of state for security assistance, science, and technology and chaired the National Security Council Group on Nonproliferation of Nuclear Weapons.

Robert E. Pendley has taught at the University of Hawaii and Rice University (1968-72), worked as a Washington consultant for the Resource Management Corporation (1972-74), and served in government with the Federal Energy Administration, where he was a division chief in the Policy and Analysis group (1974-76). In 1976 he joined the Regional Studies group at Los Alamos, in charge of constructing models for analyzing regional energy development issues. In 1980 he moved to the office of the assistant director for planning and analysis.

Joseph F. Pilat was a Philip Mosely Fellow and a special assistant to Professor Walter Laqueur at the Center for Strategic and International Studies, Georgetown University. Subsequently, he was a senior research associate in the Office of Senior Specialists, Congressional Research Service, the Library of Congress. He joined Los Alamos National Laboratory in 1983, where he is currently a staff member in the Strategic Analysis Group of the Office of the Assistant Director for Planning and Analysis. Dr. Pilat has published extensively on nuclear energy and weapons issues for British and U.S. scholarly journals, and for the U.S. Congress.

Lawrence Scheinman is professor of international law and relations at Cornell University. He was formerly the principal deputy as well as the senior advisor to the under secretary of state for security assistance, science, and technology. Previous to holding the aforementioned posts, he was responsible for international policy planning at Energy Research Development and Administration.

Henry David Sokolski is a senior aide to Senator Dan Quayle for international security affairs. He was previously a public affairs fellow at the Hoover Institution on War, Revolution, and Peace, Stanford University, as well as special assistant to Senator Gordon J. Humphrey for nuclear energy issues. He authored the Humphrey-Roth amendment to the Export Administration Act.

Leonard S. Spector is a senior associate at the Carnegie Endowment for International Peace and has worked in the field of nuclear nonproliferation for nearly ten years, first with the Nuclear Regulatory Commission and then on the staff of the Senate Energy and Nuclear Proliferation Subcommittee, where he served as chief counsel from 1978 to 1980.

Edward F. Wonder is a senior consultant with International Energy Associates Limited of Washington, D.C. Before coming to IEAL in 1978, he was a research associate in the Peace Studies Program and the Program on Science, Technology and Society at Cornell University (1976-78), and postdoctoral fellow at the School of International Affairs at Carleton University, Ottawa, Canada (1975-76).